Waterscapes

Waterscapes

A SouthCoast Anthology

by Midori Creativity & the Westport Writers Group

Waterscapes: A SouthCoast Anthology is a project of Midori Creativity and the Westport Writers Group.

Front cover image: "Held by the Horizon" by Stefanie Toner

Cover and interior book design by Lisa Ferreira, LCF Design

This project is supported in part by a grant from the Mass Cultural Council, a state agency.

ISBN 979-8-9902233-1-8

Library of Congress Control Number: 2025902551

Published by Midori Creativity, Westport, MA, USA.

midoricreativity.com

Printed in the United States of America

First Printing Edition, 2025

Table of Contents

Preface

Waterscapes

"What is a waterscape?" I ask my soft-spoken, constant, authoritative, omni-present, all-knowing AI oracle pal SIRI.

"a landscape whose dominant feature is water," she replies dryly.

Poor Siri. So sad. She has no idea…I fear for the future.

Step into space and look back at the earth—now that's a waterscape, Siri.

Thank goodness there are SouthCoast writers and photographers who will open their minds, hearts, and apertures to prove beyond a shadow of a doubt that there is a lot more to a waterscape than the absence of land.

In these pages you will find images and stories to savor: a father and his children scrambling to welcome a winter sunrise, creating memories that will be stored and passed from one generation to the next; a grandma whose father taught her to lean into the waves to deal with the turbulence of life; a boat that captures and releases a flood of lifetime memories.

Waterscapes honor wave-driven time travel where myths and magical shapes shift and unite life and the seemingly lifeless—pitching forward and back between past and future.

Waterscapes take us to far away places and timeless encounters and offer intriguing questions.

Are family summer vacations remembered more for the fishy or the family encounters?

How do we savor and share these memories with generations to come?

Can we slow down the pace of our world and emotions when we tune into the rhythms of the sea?

We think so. And we think you will, too.

by Lorna Miles

Introduction

We as a species feel a distinct call to the water, an ancient and gentle summoning. Water has always been a necessary precursor to life. Humans settle around rivers, lakes, bays, and coastlines. We build our shelters to weather the salt and sea. We are made of water. It ebbs and flows within us, reinventing our lives like the changing tide.

The same water droplets that fill the ocean quelled volcanic earth and doused prehistoric beasts. That same water filled the cup of Cleopatra and creased the face of Zheng Yi Sao. That is the water that flows now, through our ecosystem and our bodies, sustaining us and washing us clean. Many of us find great peace by the water. Others find escape along the shoreline, reposing in ways Poseidon would envy. A few of us behold a great beast of water and wave, murky visions of pale surf, the call, and the dread.

Before our feet marked the mud of these shores, the Sakonnet, Nauset, Wampanoag, and Narragansett lived, worked, and flourished in our waters. Before tea soaked the harbor and red stained the soil, these people co-existed with the land and water. Now, living within a fragile, finite ecosystem, we must learn to relate yet again. Suck in the air, taste the salt on our lips, let salt spray fill our lungs. We release that held breath and close our eyes.

In this second anthology by Midori Creativity and the Westport Writers Group, thirty local writers and photographers journey through the waters of the SouthCoast. Ponds, tidepools, raindrops. Rivers, bays, and oceans. *Waterscapes* moves us through the cycles of Moontide to Flow to Ebbtide. The imaginative writing and luminous photography highlight the vital nautical landscape of the SouthCoast, strengthening our connection to its history and ecology. Writers and artists have a unique role to play in building an essential link between appreciation of the local landscape and stewardship of our natural resources. This creative work serves to aid in building a community that recognizes the importance of protecting and preserving these natural treasures.

by Nicholas Rachel

Moon Tide

~~~~~~
~~~~~~

Winter Sunrising

Someday you may find yourself jolted out of bed in total darkness because your child has burst into your room like a freight train.

"Come play! Get up, get up, get UP!" they'll shout while tugging your sleeve. "Get up on your LEGS!"

You'll get up on your legs; there is no snooze button.

As you lumber down the stairs into the arctic cold, you'll be horrified to discover that the oven clock shows 5:05 am, just as it did yesterday and the day before that. The choice is simple: refuse to play and endure the ensuing discontent or engage in a game of "All Engines Go" for three, maybe four hours before the rest of the world wakes up.

You could consume enough coffee to propel Thomas the Tank Engine around the couch sixty to eighty times…but by noon you'd derail from a caffeine crash. You could also turn on the TV and go back to bed, but would that really invigorate you? Consider another idea: bundle up your family, go outside in the pitch black, and head to the beach by Ned's Point Lighthouse. Witness the winter sunrise.

You won't be eager to do it.

You'll be too tired because you'll have stayed up late scrolling on your phone, trying to regain a sense of freedom that escaped you during the day.

You'll be too cold because you won't yet have learned the joys of merino wool layers.

You'll be too annoyed because a four-year-old will kick and scream everywhere but in their snowsuit, and a one-year-old will need a diaper change as soon as you've buttoned their last button.

Hopefully, though, you have a life partner who is significantly wiser than you, who wants to make the most of living on the SouthCoast. Someone who wakes up early to finish knitting your hat, who pre-warms the snowsuit in the dryer, and who patiently turns getting dressed into a game about outer space.

"What if we pretend we're putting on our space suits to explore the moon?" they might suggest.

"And moon rocks will fuel all our engines!" you'll be proud to say. Your little astronaut may surrender a half-smile—sometimes you just have to reframe things.

Don't misunderstand—it will take thirty minutes to get everyone out the door, and you'll do multiple diaper changes—but you'll manage. You'll step into the brisk air and venture into the great unknown.

Once outside, it may become critical to be "on time." Not to miss the sunrise, after all that. Of course kids like to meander around the dirt path leading to the lighthouse, crunching ice or picking berries. "Hurry!" you'll say, "we don't want to miss it!"

The beach may indeed feel like outer space. No one will have set foot on the rocks where you stand for hours, maybe days. The winds are stronger than at your house; they can feel overwhelming and immense. As you step forward, you may spot a horseshoe crab shell tangled in dried seaweed or hear a seagull screech above your head as if to say, "what are you doing here?"

What are you doing here? You're not cut out for absorbing icy winds in your face. You're wearing socks on your hands because you couldn't find gloves. Worse, you could begin to anticipate the grim realities of the day ahead. You have difficult emails to write to difficult people and there won't be childcare to give you time to write them. It will just be "All Engines Go" for minute after relentless minute.

The lighthouse will pulse rhythmically, as if to announce something important. An orange glow on the horizon will appear softly at first, then will pick up its intensity. Some clouds may look cartoonishly white, ominous gray, or rosy with pink cheeks. It may not be clear why or how these patterns occur, but every color that you see will become more brilliant in its own right, until you're sure they can't possibly change any more, and they surprise you again.

You may wish to go home after the initial moment of awe. Escape the cold. Dig into those emails. Before you do, notice your child sprawled out on the sand, eyes locked on building a moat around a moon castle. See the force with which they throw rocks into the ocean to tell the sun to get UP on its legs. Imagine their wonder as they stare at the red reflection on the water, shimmering the way the moon does at night. You know you'll miss this someday; of course you will. It's a strange paradox: simultaneously wishing this moment would go by faster and also that it would never end.

As broad daylight arrives, you may see a family of ducks glide gently on the
rolling waves or hear an airplane fly overhead. After a spectacular event—
light waves radiating across water waves—life simply carries on. It's easy to
be present at the beginning and at the end; it's the middle where we grow
restless. What if you reframe things? You understand, intellectually, that
the sun will come up tomorrow and the day after that. But how would you
experience the winter sunrise if you knew it was your last? My guess is, my
children, it'd feel a lot like your first—the time you witnessed it with me.

Someday, my children,
When the days feel slow
You may find yourself stalled
Your engines won't go
Remember the beach
On Sea Marsh Way.
You may need the winter sunrise.
You may, someday.

by Aaron Smith

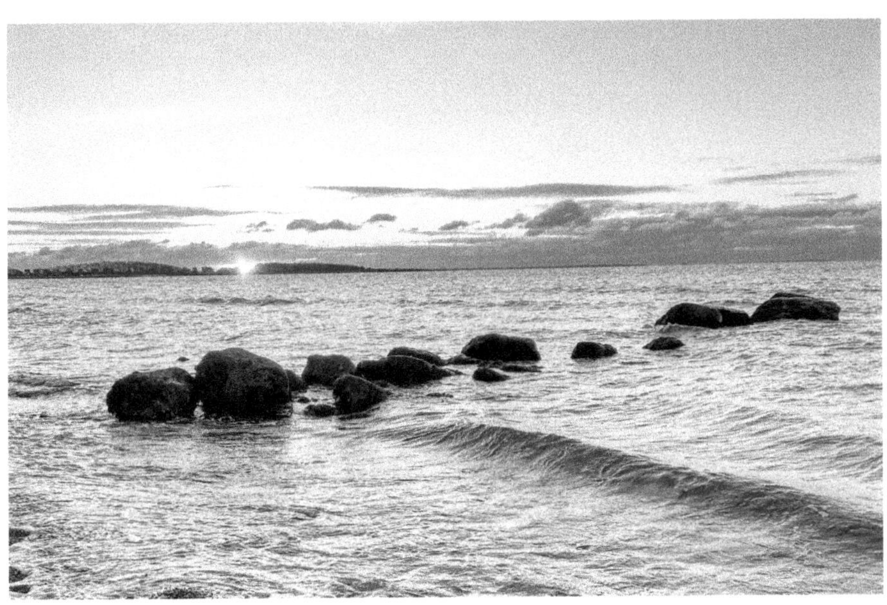

River Magic

Rivers — running, rushing, rumbling, raging
Each one shows its life within and without
Mysteries spilling over the miles of banks
Eons of history on the river floors.

Microscopic life in the silky shine of waters
Geese, ducks, loons, birds of all kinds
Are supported above the lively Westport River
We see their nests as we skim along in boats.

Observing all rivers that never stop
From where does all the water come
And to where does it continue to flow?
The power of Niagara has no answer.

All great rivers have minds of their own
When their floods overspread the connecting land
And nothing man can do will help contain
The raging waters as they wildly cross the plains.

The other extreme plays out in droughts
When rivers become a mere trickle,
Leaving the wildlife bereft and thirsty;
Man cannot control the amount of rain.

Rivers are testaments to our earth's fluidity
The water that we need to survive is held
Within the mighty troughs of rivers,
There to revere, respect, observe with awe.

by Joan V. McKinley

Going Home

Selling our home without another in the middle of the pandemic seemed like a good idea at the time.

Living in Jamaica Plain for thirty years, Dave and I loved the community with all our hearts, but our souls were longing to be closer to nature. Although we'd looked for years for a place close to woods and water to call "home," nothing clicked. As an interim measure, Dave scratched his Nature itch by buying a boat in Seattle a few years prior and sailed her to the Sea of Cortez when Covid hit.

On one of those heart-achingly beautiful, late August, blue-sky golden days in 2020, I asked myself, "HOW could it be that I was still living in the city instead of harvesting vegetables, flowers, raspberries and honey on a bucolic landscape?" I might have been reading too much zen material—the ones that tell you "Jump! And the net will appear!" but after communing with an old cherry tree in the Arnold Arboretum, I got the message, "Sell the house now and let the process unfold." So we did.

As our short-term housing unexpectedly disappeared and the real estate market skyrocketed I wondered when exactly the net was going to appear. We bought a camper van and traveled the country looking for "the place." But this was like chasing a wild horse, nothing felt right, and after six months, our travels circled us right back to…Boston. Only this time, we landed in the super-urban Fenway district.

It seemed clear that Boston wasn't done with us yet. Settling into our city space, I remained optimistic that a gentler location would be ours, while getting the message that the Universe had a patience lesson to teach. After three years of Fenway living, I started to wonder if I would ever find my place.

In the meantime, Dave continued to travel back and forth from Boston to wherever Navigator, his boat, was holed up and he was now in the final leg of the six year, non-contiguous journey. Over the years, he'd sailed Navigator from the Sea of Cortez, along Mexico's so-called "happy coast," through Central America and the Panama Canal, and was in a final run home to the Northeast.

It was May and he was in Virginia's Chesapeake Bay, looking for a New England marina to call home for the summer.

Every fiber of me envisioned us living on the boat in a quiet, charming little harbor that summer—a place I'd walk to nature trails, see stars at night, hear birds in the morning and meander to a precious little village to buy a book and an over-priced sandwich. Maybe coastal Maine.

So when Dave called me from Chesapeake Bay and told me he was bringing Navigator to New Bedford Harbor for the summer, I was not happy.

Instead of a delightful little fishing village, he was heading straight for one of the biggest, loudest, commercial fishing harbors on the East Coast. A quick Google search further informed me that New Bedford Harbor was an 18,000 square foot urban tidal estuary filled with sediment highly contaminated with PCBs and heavy metals. We'd be right next to the loud, heavy equipment of the dredging clean-up crew.

"What?! New Bedford?! Why?!" I asked. "WHAT are you thinking? How about Maine?"

Trying to negotiate with a boat captain who's been at sea for six months is like talking to a whale. Not only was he used to having the final word for everything, he was also tuned in to a higher consciousness from living in the elements, connected to every sunrise, sunset, the sea and sky. I say "higher consciousness;" he would call it "woo."

"Ok—what about Westport? Padanaram? Wickford? Maine?" I asked, a little desperate.

"Everything is booked or too expensive. I'm going to New Bedford. I got the last slip in the cheapest marina," was his three-sentence communication.

I wanted precious. He wanted cheap.

I love this husband of thirty years, but his Scottish frugality was just too much this time and when I hung up the phone, the thought bubble, "You're an A-Hole," appeared.

Still, it was better than an asphalt jungle in July, so I packed my bag and some groceries and headed to New Bedford Harbor. The hammering of the dredging clean-up crew drowned out the birdsong, while the all-night commercial lights obscured any chance of star-gazing, but the briny salt air and epic sunsets were still balm for my soul.

Navigator had just completed an 8000-mile journey and was in need of maintenance and repairs, so instead of sailing off to explore Buzzards Bay, we stayed tied up in the marina with the dredging crew.

Vacillating between feeling incredibly lucky to be on the water and trying not to harbor resentment for my husband's insistence on this industrial dock was a daily balancing act.

One hot and steamy August morning, with no pristine nature trails nor charming tree-lined village with cafés selling over-priced sandwiches remotely in sight, my resentment barometer ratcheted up.

I would go to yoga to cool down. Driving through crowded industrial New Bedford to the yoga studio on a hot summer day, I questioned the wisdom of this choice and nearly turned back. But something nudged me on.

Entering the Power and Grace yoga studio, I felt my whole body relax. Something immediately clicked and the energy, light and…magic of the place infused me with a bone-deep knowing that I'd found my people, my place. It was like…I was home.

Serendipity quickly unfolded with almost ridiculous ease as I immersed myself in the community. While I still wasn't exactly sure why I was hanging out in industrial New Bedford when I said I wanted quiet and charming, here we now were, buying an enchanted home 2 blocks to the sea in Fairhaven so I could be connected to these people, the water, and the woods. I had found my place.

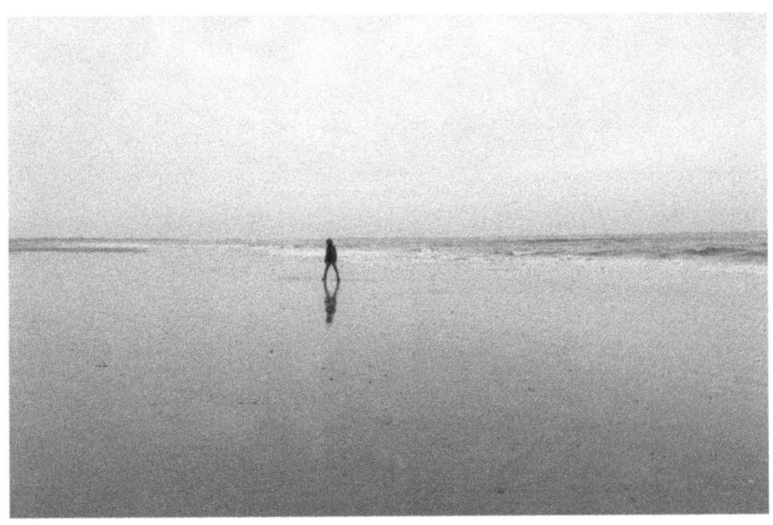

Alone Not Lonely by Krista Allen

Some say the Universe always gives us what we need, even when we don't know it. Maybe especially when we don't know it. Usually when we're looking the other way.

Talking over dinner one evening, I ate a little crow and acknowledged to Dave that I'd been wrong to give him a hard time for choosing New Bedford.

Dave got quiet for a long time and then softly revealed that when he was a day out from New Bedford, the largest pod of sea life he had ever seen in sixty years appeared out of nowhere. Dolphins surrounded his boat—hundreds of playful dolphins, with large pods of whales in the distance, escorting, guiding, swimming them home.

None of the crew had ever seen anything like it. I could see how moved he was in the remembering and re-telling of it.

Although most dolphins will swim with a boat for a short period, these welcome-dolphins swam with them through the day. And when Dave and Navigator made the turn into New Bedford harbor, their dolphin guides turned and swam away.

What do you make of this? Is it coincidence? Or is there a greater force we're all connected to when we slow down and tune in to the rhythm of the Sea? A homing force that can guide us towards what our hearts most want and need?

What I know is that living close to nature—either on sea or land—can open our intuition and sixth sense, connecting us to the life force in everything, if we let it. It can allow us to "see around corners," tap into wisdom, and guide us home.

Things are not always as they appear, are they? While I was looking in the other direction, Dave could see around corners from living at sea. He could see where home was.

by Diane Pienta

Glide

Living near the water, I feel the weather in my bones
And as I age, I find a longing to return to the sea
Not to drown, but to glide—naked on next moontide
Thoughtless, silent, and free

by Eve Lesses

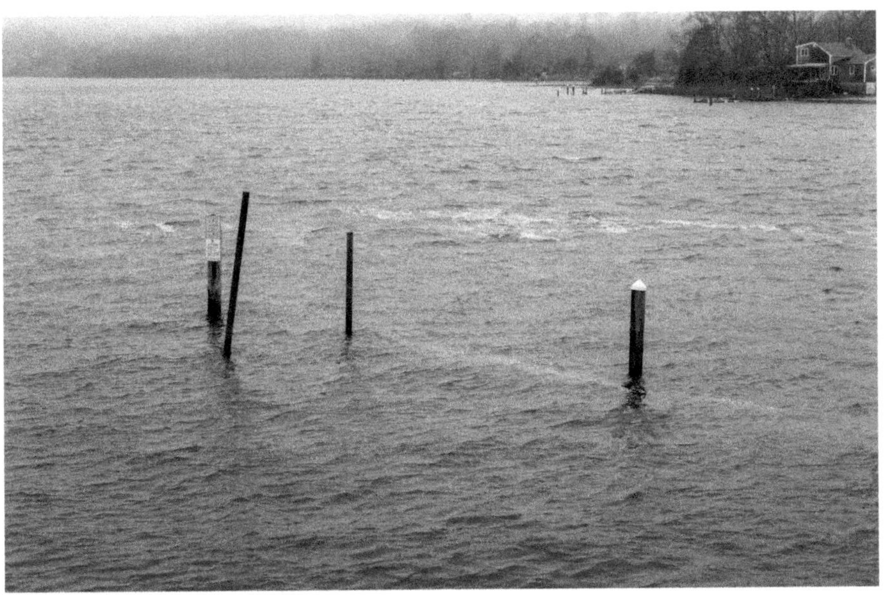

Moontide by Midori Evans

"Emelia, jump! Now!" said Hector, my brother. His fingers were hot and sweaty, grasping my hand until he let go. I leaped from the dock to a boat. One of my legs plunged into the cold waves, and the other leg caught onto the boat. A hand clamped my arm, tight, yanking me over the gunwale, swinging me as the water streamed from my clothes and knapsack.

"Christ, kid, you stupid," a man shouted. "You don't land in the sea! Here, here on the deck!" He stomped his foot and pushed me aside. I tripped on a rope that was slung onto the deck as the boat pushed away from the dock and motored into the current. Was I the last? Was the man waiting for me?

Men and women were huddled under the running lights. I crawled into a space next to them.

"Make yourself small," a woman hissed. She brushed against me but shoved me away because my clothes were wet. I shivered, cramped between a rope and the muttering voice. I squeezed the knapsack under my legs. She slapped my head if I leaned into her whenever the boat lurched. Where were we? Past the stone barricade at the edge of the harbor?

The running lights disappeared under a wall of water, everywhere a black bubble. The waves rose above the deck; sea spray and vomit were flung at me. I began to sing: *I am a fish. I swim in the harbor. I am Emelia.* As I nodded into sleep, my head bounced against the woman's arm.

"Oh, you are a child. What are you doing here?" she whispered. "It is too dangerous for you, a little girl, and for us."

"Hector is my brother," I said. "This is what he told me to do." But the woman did not hug me the way Mama did when I obeyed.

My trousers and blouse were stiff with cold. The sea was a giant spray, booming up, up, rippling and glowing with a strange light. Everyone was tucked against their knees, burrowed into the sides of the boat away from the water that swept across the deck. It could lash out at us and send everyone overboard. I strained to hear a voice, someone calling—*Emelia*—above the roar of the engine.

Weeks before tonight Hector had promised to take me to the shrimp boat, a new one in the fleet. As the sun began to set, we were finally on our way to the harbor where he moored the vessel.

"What color did you paint the hull?" I asked him.

"Blue, Mama's favorite, with an orange stripe," he said.

"I like pink," I said.

"I know," he said. "The deckhouse is pink." He laughed.

"I'm ten years old now," I said. "I can be first mate." I clapped my hands and whistled a tune.

The cab of his truck smelled of diesel. After he parked, he wrapped a blanket around my knees. It was damp with a bitter odor, thick, like smoke.

"Sh-h-h," he said. "Stop talking, stop singing. Stop asking your questions. Sh-h-h. You are Hector's little sister, so you will work hard. Not as a deck-hand. You are too smart. I have to look after Mama. But you have to leave. There's nothing here for a bright girl like you. Go to America. Be a doctor and come home to care for her." He rubbed my neck and draped the blanket over my head like a hood. He carried me in his arms as he had done when I was a small child. He was breathing heavily as if he had been running. My legs were so long they dangled against his. At the dock he hugged me and set me down, away from him, close to a boat with an engine off its stern.

"Where's the pink deckhouse?" I asked as he pulled the blanket off my shoulders.

He grinned, the way he used to surprise me in a game. Then he lifted me, grasping my fingers in his. His heart pounded right into my ribs. "Hector!" I shouted when his hand let go.

Why Hector? Why did he give me to these people? He was Mama's best; he didn't leave like the other brothers—Luis, Bernardo, Rafael. Now I have gone, too, from him and Mama—but where? To live with Luis? He was so much older that I don't know him. Would he even remember me? Or Bernardo—he loved horses. The neighbor's farm had only one mule in the field. Maybe Bernardo left to find horses. And Rafael—he scared Mama with his rage. Please, Hector, do not send me to live with him!

In my sleep I listened to the gears of the engine shifting. The boat lunged forward, settled and rocked side to side. The woman next to me pulled my arm to stand up, and we stood in line. We leaped overboard into the surf. Saltwater filled my mouth as a wave closed over my head. My feet hit the sandy bottom. Coughing and sputtering, I struggled to breathe. I followed a man whose wet shirt glistened in the sunlight. My head bobbed, choking as the water buried me. The man grabbed me. He yanked me through the waves, clamped against his hip, all the way to a beach. White clouds rose through the trees; their leaves diminished the sun. Cold was in my bones, paralyzing me, or was it hunger? Grains of sand stuck to my tongue. I threw up and choked, again and again. I crawled onto shore. Sand and trees everywhere to heaven.

by Margot Green

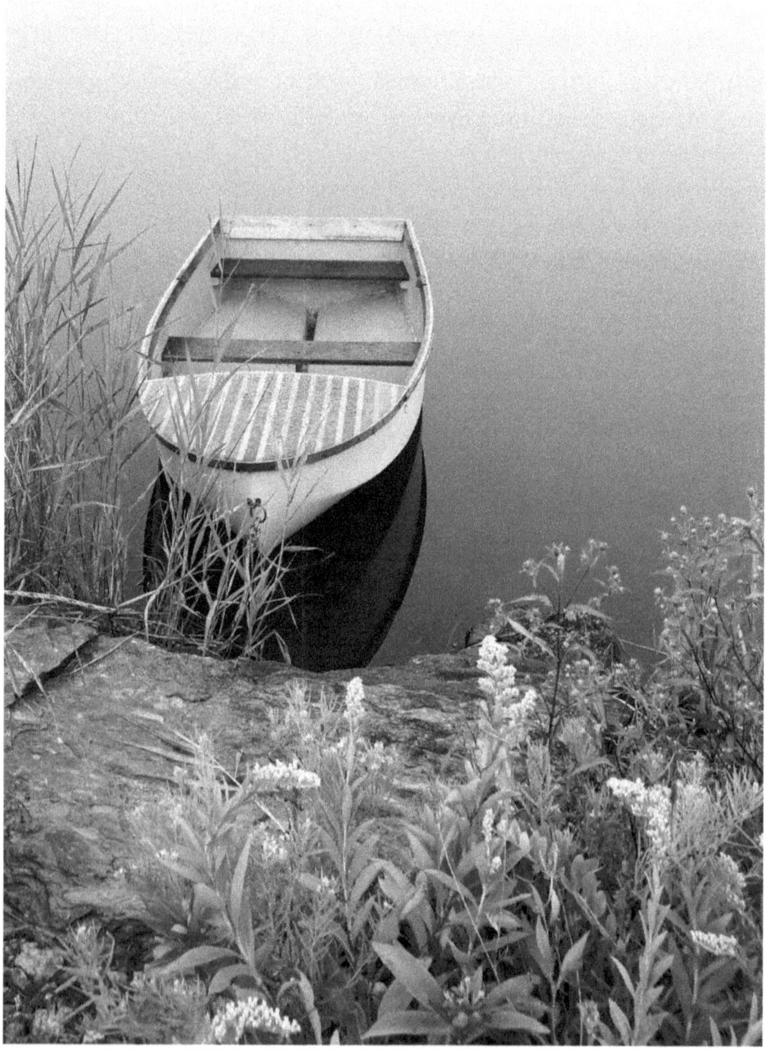

Hejira by Melinda Green

Hold Down

Gravity surrenders its grasp.
Air is forced out of my lungs
As I tumble
Through surf
Upside down
Tossed about
As easily as a piece of seaweed.

What feels like an eternity
Ten seconds or less
That's how time works
Between waves
The sets on a good day
Coming at intervals of
Eight
Ten
Twelve seconds or longer
A long time to hold your breath
When you aren't expecting to have to
Air already expelled.

My buoyant body
Breaches the surface
I open my eyes
To another wave
Bearing down
Curling
Closing over my head.

I gasp
Inhale
A shallow breath
A partial refill
Before plunging back under.

My board is whipped away
Over the falls
Pulling me with it
Somersaulting again
Weightless
Yet simultaneously heavy
My lungs burning with effort
To ignore the instinct
To open my nose and mouth
For relief.

I rise
Above the water once more.
Sucking oxygen
Quickly
Deeply
As the third wave of the set approaches.

Diving down again
Swimming under
Like a duck
Expelling a trail of bubbles
Dragging my board along
Into the cold
The depths
The darkness.

This is how I'll die.

My lungs will fill with fluid
Water which makes life possible
May define my longevity
Ending everything in a moment.

But not today
As I emerge
Yanking the board towards me
Climbing back on
A fluid, practiced motion
Clinging to life
On repeat.

by Krista Allen

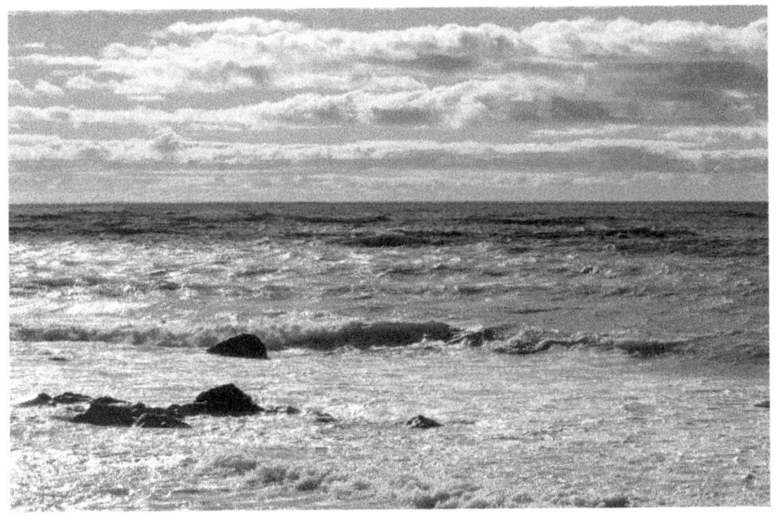

Windwater Streaming by Midori Evans

My Apprenticeship at the Islands

Surely, I thought to myself, there is no more beautiful place in the world. The year was 1968, and I was still in high school, but through an improbable string of events I found myself in Robinson's Hole in an unseaworthy skiff with an elderly gentleman at the helm.

It all started in Siam in the late 1940's. My grandmother was concerned when my father suddenly disappeared from his dorm at Brown University and was not mollified in the least when she got a telegram from my dad saying he was boarding a tramp steamer for the Far East. My dad bounced around Southeast Asia and eventually ended up with a job as a reporter for the English language newspaper in Bangkok. It was here that he met a remarkable Renaissance man by the name of Gordon Browne. Gordon grew up in Marion, MA, studied anthropology at Harvard, played strong safety on their football team, and did archaeological work in Morocco with his professor, Carlton Coon. At the outbreak of WWII, he was recruited by the OSS for intelligence work in Morocco. At the time, Morocco was a swirling caldron of Vichy, Free French, Nazi, Spanish, Berber, American, and British intrigue; Gordon loved it. After the war, Browne worked in various "diplomatic," i.e. intelligence, posts in places such as India, Yemen, Borneo, and Siam where he met my father. Gordon "collected" interesting people and naturally befriended my eccentric father.

After Gordon retired, he got a multi-year rental of a villa in Tangier, Morocco in a fine location overlooking the Strait of Gibraltar. In the meantime his daughter, Akeeyah Bourgoin, bought a house in Woods Hole, Massachusetts. Gordon spent the off season in Morocco (where we visited him) but migrated to the Hole every fall to fish for striped bass along the Elizabeth Islands and socialize with his old OSS associates and some of his colorful friends, including my father.

And so it was that the elderly Gordon Browne took me under his wing, and we became fast friends; I suppose I was part of his collection, having inherited some of my dad's quirks. I was but a wee lad, still in a protracted larval stage, and obsessed with fishing. When Gordon took me out in his ancient and very dubious skiff, the Mummichaug, I thought I was in heaven; this was so much better than chasing tiny, recalcitrant brook trout in the Beaver River in Rhode Island. I wanted to learn everything I could about striped bass and the ocean. Unlike my time in school, I eagerly absorbed every lesson that Gordon taught me.

Gordon had the Mummichaug tied up at Dan Clark's dock in Eel Pond in Woods Hole. On a typical fishing day, we would slowly motor out over the pond, always on the lookout for menhaden to use as bait, and pass under the Water Street bridge (we could scrunch down and wiggle under the bridge— our boat was too small to rate a bridge opening) and on to the Hole proper. From here Gordon would gun the engine, and we would skim across the vexed and treacherous waters of this infamous passage. Gordon seemingly did not pay much attention to channel markers, reefs, or rips; the Mummi-chaug blithely skipped across it all as I stared down into the depths in awe. We would traverse bottomless green holes and then suddenly the depth would come up to a few feet and I could see menacing rocks with medusan locks of writhing seaweed and then in an instant, we were back over the emerald depths. The Mummichaug was so tiny, a mote to Neptune's eye, that the sea demons that inhabited the Hole could not be bothered wrecking it. But woe be to the foolish fishermen in their big plastic boats who tried to follow us; more than one copycat ended up bouncing off a rock.

One morning, after skimming over the Hole, Gordon dropped the anchor and announced that we were at Pine Island to try for some huge bluefish that had been terrorizing these waters. To me, Pine Island was just a bunch of slimy rocks that barely showed at low tide, but Gordon explained that when he was young, it was a real island with pine trees; he used to picnic there. The Hurricane of '38 had reduced it to its current humble state. This deeply impressed me, for here was a man who had experienced geological time, but this was just the beginning; Gordon gradually educated me, better than any teacher in my classrooms. He showed me how glaciers had built Cape Cod and the Islands but explained how the ocean was gradually reclaiming the land. The Cape and the Islands were built on fluff; as Gordon said with a smirk, everyone who lives on Cape Cod will eventually have waterfront! Of great interest to me was a bluff that Gordon pointed out; as he explained it, Tertiary and even late Cretaceous fossils could be found here eroding out of the deposits. Cretaceous as in dinosaurs, I asked? No, just Cretaceous marine invertebrates ploughed up by the glaciers into large hummocks that the ocean was nibbling away at, exposing layers of clay, gravel, greensand, and even lignite coal.

Gradually, under Gordon's tutelage, I began to lift my eyes from the wa-ter and see the world beyond. On each trip he would make sure I noticed the bits and pieces that fit together in a connected natural world along the islands. He pointed out the whirlwinds of tree swallows twisting over the bay-berry bushes along the shore of the Elizabeth Islands. He explained that they

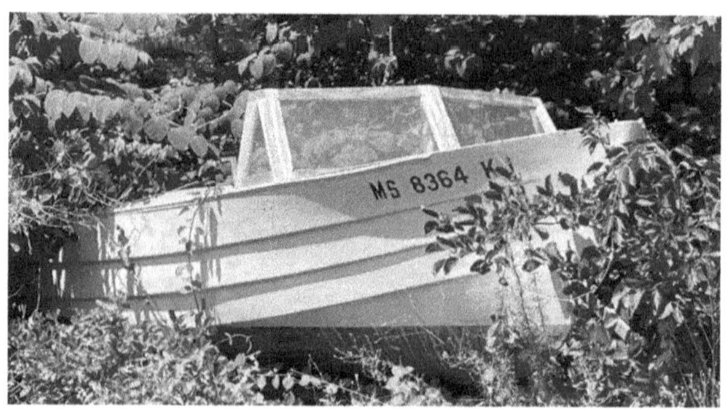

Mummichaug by Sam Dennis

could digest the waxy coating of the bayberries and in exchange for this gift, they would reseed the islands along the way. One morning a vigorous bird on scimitar wings flashed past us; Gordon explained that this was a peregrine falcon on the lookout for shorebirds on its way south during migration. On some trips we would go ashore and harvest beach plums for Akeeyah's delicious beach plum jam. Gordon's insatiable curiosity about the natural world and his delight in human diversity were the most important lessons for me.

Back then, the islands were a delightful window into a forgotten, rural past with open meadows, stone walls, and flocks of sheep trotting this way and that. It was the most magical land I had ever seen; Gordon knew the trustees, and we would visit various friends on these enchanted islands.

One afternoon we stopped at Pasque Island to have lunch with the caretakers, Barbara and Heydt, on their lonely sea girt outpost. They lived in a swayed back cottage built from ship timbers and driftwood. Planted in the yard was the wooden sailing dinghy that Heydt had built on Tuckernuck and used to get to Pasque; I guess Tuckernuck was getting too urban for them! Heydt was skilled at wooden boat building and even wrote a symphony or two. He showed me his locally famous barn; it was full of all sorts of odds and ends that he had found on the shore including wooden spars, planks, and blocks from the Age of Sail; the ocean only grudgingly gave up its treasures gathered a century ago. But what really impressed me was our conversations, if you could call them that; we could not get a word in edgewise; they seemed starved for human society and poured out a continuous stream of stories. To my young, impressionable mind, Heydt and Barbara made me think of castaways such as Alexander Selkirk or even Treasure Island's Ben Gun. And maybe that was not too far fetched since these islands, as Gordon explained, were frequented by pirates. In fact, Gordon told me that he'd had a picnic at Quick's Hole with a resident of the islands and dug up a human skeleton without a skull and an ancient boot held together with wooden pegs.

It was not just the islands and the local waters that so fascinated me. The town of Woods Hole was a wild, woolly, and romantic place back then. I frequently saw an eccentric young man named Billy riding an old fashioned high-wheel bicycle playing a flute; this was Woods Hole, so no one so much as raised an eyebrow. Gordon was fond of telling everyone about the impression of a stout young man who had been thrown against the wall of the Captain Kidd bar. Only much later did I find out that his daughter Akeeyah would sometimes dance on the tables at the Captain Kidd.

After our fishing trips, Dan Clark would pull us into his quaint ship chandlery to hear what was happening on the water and ply us with a finger or two of excellent rum which our dehydrated bodies readily accepted. Then we would stumble down Millfield Street to Akeeyah's house to have dinner and another drink or two (hot buttered rums if we were cold) and then to bed. Those were glorious fishing adventures indeed, but Gordon did so much more to expand my horizons. He made it a habit of introducing me to various scientists and peculiar personalities. We had dinner with the likes of John Buck (who regaled us with his research into synchronous fireflies), Jim Mavor (who helped develop the Alvin submersible), Alan Poole (who was working with ospreys), Frank Mather (bluefin tuna researcher), and many more characters.

Over the years fishing with Gordon and others, I developed a deep concern about the future of striped bass and got involved in the so-called Striper Wars of the 1980's. Gordon was very supportive of my efforts. While Gordon introduced me to many intriguing people in Woods Hole, my involvement with striped bass advocacy introduced me to a whole new circle of friends. My work eventually led me to a commune on Martha's Vineyard where I had lunch with Thomas Hart Benton's daughter Jessie; to my star-struck eyes, this young lady seemed like the embodiment of Tolkien's Goldberry.

Gordon lived to be 93 years old; he and most of his friends are now gone, but those island adventures still stick with me. When I first started visiting Gordon in Woods Hole, Cape Cod was a wild, sandy expanse of fragrant pitch pine. Not any more. While Byron wrote that, "Man marks the earth with ruin—his control Stops with the shore," in our neck of the woods, Man has marked Cape Cod with his ruin, but the devastation stops at Woods

Hole. The islands still have the magic that I first experienced there, and hopefully they will stay that way. Large numbers of war-wagon style sports fishing boats now scour the shore looking for gamefish, and greedy developers eye these islands hoping to extend their devastation to the last bastion of the wild Cape of my youth, but so far the islands have been preserved.

I goofed off after college taking various dubious jobs, just enough money to fish with. I guess I was a striper bum. Eventually I pupated and went to Brown University, but I did not run off on an adventure in the Far East as my father did; I had already had my adventure.

These days when I travel on the ferry over to Martha's Vineyard to visit my botanical friend Peter Norris, I always take a long poignant look at the Devil's Foot reef; this was Gordon's favorite fishing spot in Woods Hole. Part of Gordon still dwells on this reef since we spread his ashes there. The bold little Mummichaug still exists, although she has been up on blocks in a boat yard in Falmouth for a decade. Gordon's grandson has offered it to me. I plan to visit her next spring to pay my respects. I am not sure she will float, freighted down with so many memories as she is, but it would do my soul good to try. It would certainly make a statement among the tarted-up, six-figure, Clorox-bottle, sportfishing war wagons on the Westport River.

by Frederick Thurber

Flow

Seaside Experiences on the Wheel of the Year

The Waves That Held My Family

Black Dog beach we call it, with the frequent presence of the many Labrador Retrievers that populate the neighborhood. Decades of family get-togethers, frisbee, body surfing, and picnic lunches with "sandy" sandwiches. Over the decades, mother ocean holds us all in her warm summer embrace, bringing camaraderie and unity to the families, friends, and neighbors we are blessed to have association with, at our sunny haven at the end of Route 88.

Twilight Union of September Sun and Moon

We often choose to walk the beach after dinner, especially during a full moon on an early fall eve. The sun's light fades over Acoaxet as we view the western horizon from Baker's Beach, where the magnified glowing orange moon appears to the east over Gooseberry Island. As the Moon ascends, a shaft of orange light glimmers across the bight of the three-mile-long expanse of Horseneck. The beauty of this ephemeral scene imbues a warm quietude into our hearts and minds.

November's First Gale on Gooseberry Island

When the warmth of summer fades and daylight hours grow shorter, the winds of November arrive as temperatures drop. The first Nor'easter pattern develops offshore and begins to build the swell heights. With a straight southerly blow in full swing, both sides of Gooseberry Island receive 4 to 6 foot swells. The cooler water turns light brown as the higher sustained winds agitate the sea near the shore. On the east side of the island, 5 foot breakers 300 yards in length stream in from Buzzards Bay, surging upon the rocky shoreline to fill the pools and crags between boulders and rocks. On the western side, the waves reach 6 feet as they smash upon the beach terrain. The roar of the ocean and chill of the cold wind awaken one to nature's power and fury. The wavetops curl and foam as they race to the awaiting shoreline, to crash with greater power due to the steeper angle of the beach head. Waves break over Spindle Rock and further out on the ledge as the windblown sea thrashes the shoreline. Seagulls struggle to stay level as they push into the wind, while the dune grass swings wildly with the incessant gusts.

A Caucus of Seagulls

Sheltered from the wind, with the waters at Little Beach now flat and calm, on this last good December day of the year, the gulls enjoy a restful time bathing in the sun's warmth. Their white feathers glisten as they float together in the warmer shallows at the water's edge. This stretch of the beach, which sees very little human activity in winter, provides the perfect venue for the gulls to sequester themselves from boats as well as human passersby. In this isolation they are free to express themselves loudly, creating cacophonous sounds in unison. Their gathering is likely motivated by the imminent abrupt drop in both air and sea water temperatures that coincides with the rapidly approaching shortest days of the year. One can imagine their discussion to be an exchange of valuable information about where the remaining schools of fish are to be found or the whereabouts of quahogs and mussels more easily scavenged. As the food supply becomes scarcer in winter, competition gives way to cooperation. Seagulls are often observed quarreling over scrounged treasures like the washed-up remains of an overturned horseshoe crab, or in the heat of summer, a stray french fry snatched from a beach blanket. But on this day there is a feeling of alliance in their seaside caucus.

Frozen Salt

After a fortnight of freezing weather, ice forms on the Westport River's salty shores, just after the new year has commenced. Early morning sunlight reflects off the frozen sheen which has formed at the water's edge. The deeper, not yet frozen water of the channel remains flat and calm due to the absence of wind. While the scene is tranquil, the dearth of aquatic life, no longer present at the frigid shoreline, imparts a longing for the warmer seasons to come, when the crabs, minnows, and mollusks will return. Icebound rocks and shells glisten, rooted in the glaze, while their colored surfaces are magnified, revealing intricate patterns that normally go unnoticed. Winter's deepest cold brings gifts like these, unseen on summer days, with crystal clear water where every detail of the river's bottom can be seen at a 20 foot depth. Hidden gems like mooring chains, as well as boulders adorned with rockweed that rest on a light sandy bottom, are revealed. The submerged terrain is peppered with hermit crabs, while the billowing bright green eelgrass descends down into the channel from the shallows, shifting and waving in the undulating current.

by Mark L. Collins

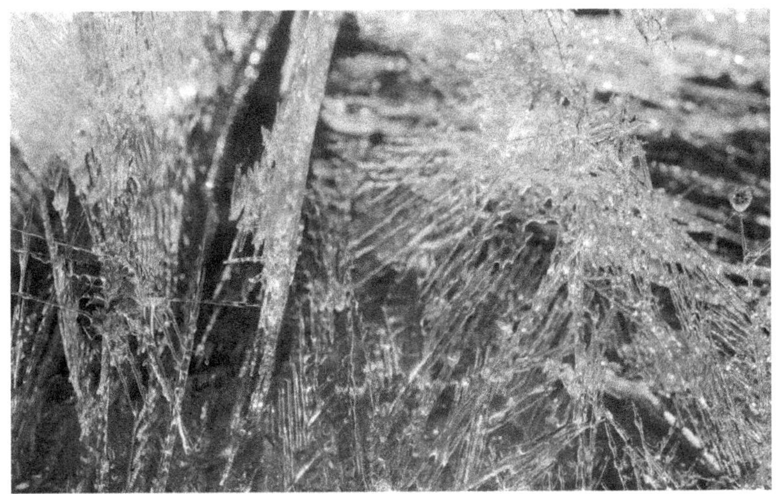

Crystalline by Midori Evans

In the Brook

The street where I grew up as a child was a magical place. There were two families and thirteen children that lived there at the top of the hill on Berryman Street, so everyone always had a playmate of sorts for any wild idea that came beckoning. It was surrounded by acres of forest at the top and a flowing brook at the bottom. The brook pooled into an overgrown marshy area, where the swamp became our own private place away from the world. When our small house got too crowded for the six kids, my mother sent us outside. I'm not even sure if words were exchanged. We just understood that our playground for the day was the great outdoors as long as we were within yoo-hooing distance.

In the forest, there were tall White Pines with lots of branches for climbing. It was a long, sappy struggle to get to the top, but from that perch, I got a bird's eye view into our neighbors' yards along Route 6. A broken branch could mean a certain death, but no one thought about that at the time. All we knew is that kids climbed trees and daring each other to climb higher was just part of the excitement. Lying about here or there on the forest floor were fallen trees leaning at precarious angles but perfect to practice the skill of beam walking. Our favorite was the enormous cuckoo tree. I'm not sure how it got that name, but its fall created an earthy dark cave perfect to shelter in

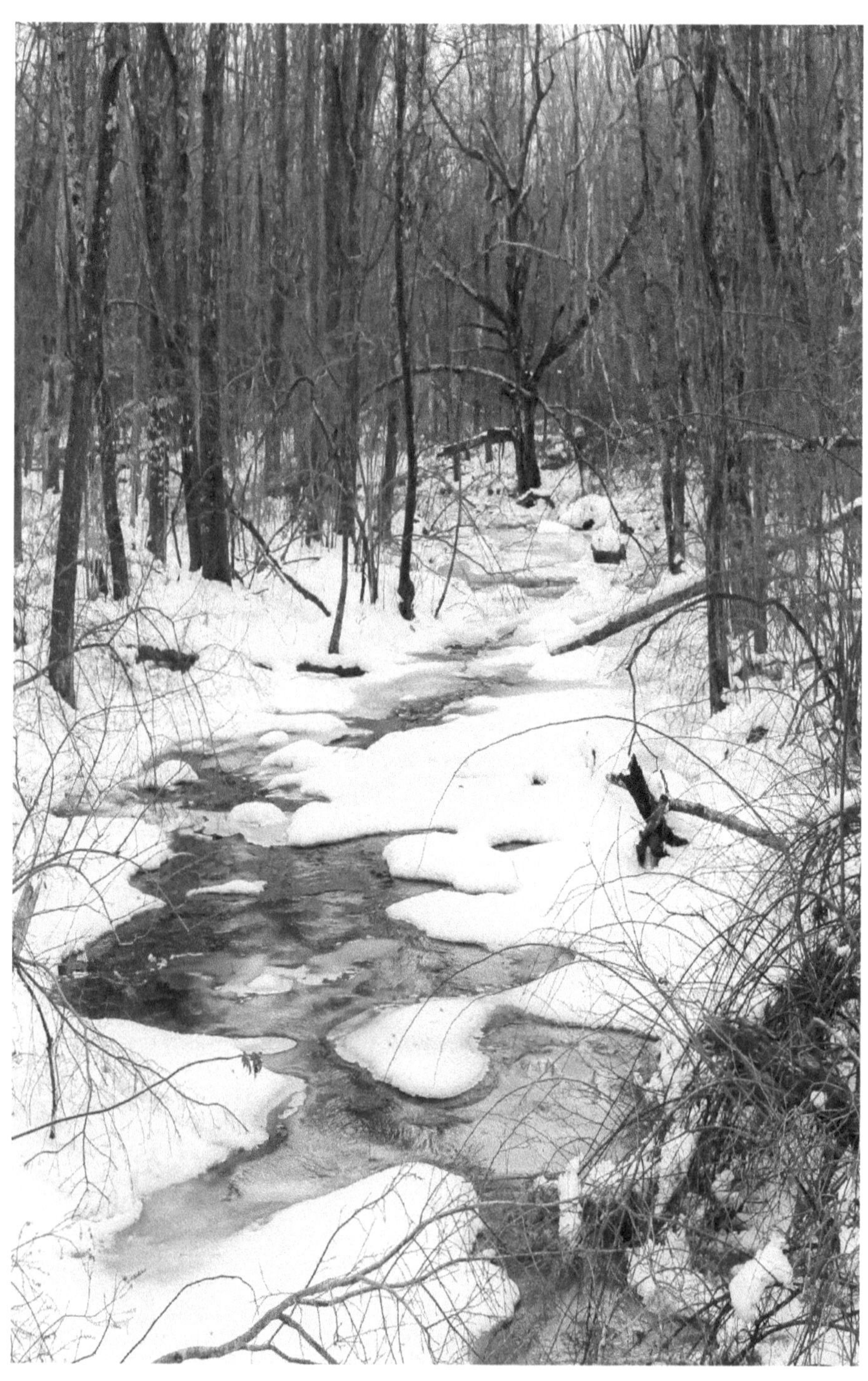

Cold Flow by Shara Grant

during hide and seek games. I can still feel that tense excitement as footsteps neared, and I can still smell the dampness of wood and humus while I waited to be discovered.

And then there was the brook, our favorite playground of all. In the winter, when the water froze, we skidded along on its smooth surface in our buckled rubber boots lined with Wonder Bread plastic bags for extra protection. It was inevitable that a thin crisp patch of ice would break through sucking in the foot, rubber boot, and plastic bag all in one quick swoop. In the spring, after the snow melted, the waters were their best, fresh and clear. We waded through the cold, marshy muck gathering squishy pollywogs in buckets in the hope of watching them hatch into tadpoles in the makeshift zoo we kept in our neighbor's backyard. We maneuvered our way through a jungle of swamp maples, tripping over fallen mossy logs in search of salamanders for our collection. Soon crickets and grasshoppers would be captured to join the menagerie we housed in a series of glass jars. We were zookeepers, or so we thought at the time. It seemed that our days on that dead end street in North Westport would go on forever, but time had a different plan for us.

As the years went by, many came to Westport to seek refuge from the hustle of city life, and businesses along the busy State Road grew in response to accommodate the many. The abandoned business at the end of our street that was once our hideout became a used car dealership with a parking lot paved right to the edge of our swamp. The small brook that was our world became smaller as the years went by or maybe it was that we just grew our way out of the 1960's. It was just one small tributary of many that together fed into the Bread and Cheese Brook on its way to the Westport River and the great Atlantic beyond. Back when we plunged our hands into the ice-cold stream in search of the elusive catch of the day, we were blissfully unaware of the riots and protests marching across our country. We didn't understand the news about a war being fought in a faraway land, but the hours on the clock slowly ticked on and with it our childhood. As the years passed, the swamp seemed to shrink in importance as the challenges of adulthood loomed ever larger. We reluctantly stepped forward to meet them, leaving the days of carefree play in the brook behind. What is left are the memories carefully tucked away in that special place in our brain where we hold the best.

by Deb Coderre

Petrichor

Driving into Little Compton in the dead of winter, along twisting back roads, you pass a small farm stand with its oysters for sale sign propped against the building. It's a little reminder, in case you're not aware of the fact, that you are in a coastal community.

As you turn on to Peckham Road, you are enveloped in farmland, which feels green, even in January or February. Eventually you hit the crest of a hill where a great vista opens before you. Big sky. Cows wading in a pond across West Main Road. Down the gently sloping hills lies the Sakonnet River. This is not just any river; it's a tidal river, an estuary. The river stretches as far as the eye can see, infusing the landscape with its own special light. In this moment you feel the spirit of the coast.

I often find myself driving those back roads in February to feel the promise of spring as the hours of daylight begin to slowly conquer the hours of darkness. I'm headed to a cluster of quaint old buildings, Peckham's Greenhouse, owned by Rick and Laura Peckham. The spring equinox is almost upon us. As I pull into a diagonal parking space, just seeing the fence and the empty tables brings memories of the gardens in summer bursting with life and color. The smell of moist earth surrounding us makes me catch my breath. I recall the bubbling fountains which seem to spring forth from the earth itself.

Peckham's offers relief from the angst of winter. By the front door, a witch hazel is in full bloom, bold and hardy in the chill of winter. Rick is always there, ready to take my carefully chosen bunch of blossoms and greens, and with his touch, render them breathtakingly beautiful. There are hundreds of little garden shops spread all over New England, but Peckham's Greenhouse rises above the rest. It's Rick's touch that fills every nook and cranny with the unexpected and delightful. He is the soul of Peckham's.

The massive bougainvillea falling over a fountain trickling into a stone-lined pool, looking like it was designed by nature, transports me to the tropics. I stand there, breathing in their fragrance, marveling at the intricacy of the delicate, tissue paper blossoms, gently touching only one. The sound of the falling water calms me and I lose track of time. Water is soothing, healing, the life blood of the planet and it permeates this space. Besides light and color and texture, the greenhouse is filled with happiness. The men and women

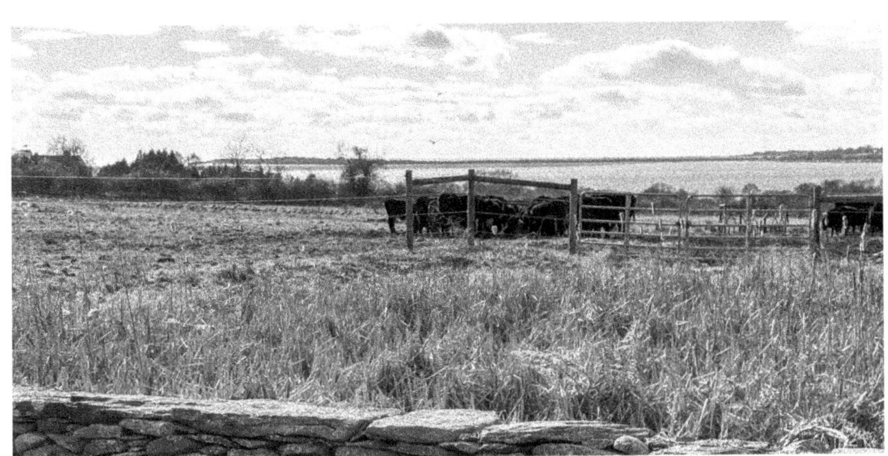

working there love plants as much as Rick. He's a fifth generation horticulturalist and the enthusiasm of Rick and his daughter Carley and his son Max is contagious.

This particular day, I need a few small water-retaining planters for my papyrus. I know where to find them and it is not Amazon, thank you very much, but the back rooms of Peckham's. There will be numerous choices. I stroll through the cavernous, ancient alley of plants that are not for sale, some 100 years old; they've been lovingly cultivated for so long. The very walls seem to ooze moisture, nurturing the moss which lines everything. The longevity of the living fauna makes me aware of my brief sojourn on this earth.

When I need to smell moist earth in the dead of winter, this is where I hail. Time is suspended. I drift and breathe and wander. In many places, there is earth under my feet, moss sprouting on craggy outcroppings, unpredictable twists and turns, passages formed organically over many years. Nothing is standard, nothing is conventional. There are no automatic doors, no set dimensions. It is like slipping into a primordial enclave, not touched by human hands. And it's Rick's sense of the organic which guides his hand, as he is led by the flora. May the Peckham family carry this on into the future, a healing gift to the whole South Coast.

by Susan Czernicka

Tuna

It's hard to imagine my parents—remembered mainly as the rule-enforcing martinets my teenage self thought they were—as ever having been young and adventurous. But deep memory tells me that they were.

We were still camping in the Holiday Rambler travel trailer, before we graduated to a tent trailer. We were seven: three little girls, Mom and Dad, my grandmother, and Hildy, our dachshund. The oldest, I must have been about ten or eleven. We were moored at our favorite Cape Cod campground in Brewster.

That afternoon, settling at our favorite little-frequented bay beach, we found something unusual: two giant yellowfin tuna, dead of course, beached on the damp, low tide sand. We girls circled the beasts, touching their slippery black sides, peering into their enormous blank eyes. Lying on their sides, their fins were as high as our heads. Sand flies billowed around the carcasses. They smelled ripely of seawater and old fish. Mom and Dad, also fascinated, speculated about how they got there.

From our spot on the beach, we could see fishing weirs out in the deep waters of the bay. These are nets set in a circular pattern with a small entrance and small bait fish within. They are designed to entrap large fish, who swim in after the bait and who then cannot get out. Later, fishing boats arrive and haul the big fish aboard, an easier catch than line fishing in the open ocean. These fish must have been caught in the weirs and brought to the beach for later retrieval. I remember being amazed at the connection between the tuna sandwiches we sometimes had for lunch and these humongous animals.

As we milled around, poking at the fish in wonderment, a man appeared and identified himself as a tuna boat captain. Why were the fish on our beach? Mom and Dad, perhaps wisely, didn't ask. They did ask about the process of fishing, told the man they were teachers, and leapt at his suggestion that they come along the next day to see for themselves how it was done. They would meet him at Rock Harbor at an ungodly hour, three or four in the morning, and he would bring them aboard.

We had often driven to Rock Harbor in the evenings to watch the fishing boats come in and hoist up their catches to be weighed—I vaguely remember tuna as large as 900 pounds, six feet long or longer. Today, tuna are so overfished that they rarely reach that size. I don't think weir fishing is legal any more; at least I haven't seen a weir at the Cape for at least thirty years.

Early Morning in Marion Harbor by Ed Reiss

The plan was that Grandma would stay with us while Mom and Dad joined the tuna fishermen on the high seas.

And so it happened. None of us were awake when Mom and Dad crept out of the trailer. Grandma and the dog snored away, prepared to make breakfast while my parents were out fishing. But no, it did not happen. They were back before dawn. I don't remember if they went back to snooze for a while; I was sleeping the deep sleep of childhood.

Having arrived at the dock at the appointed hour, Mom and Dad learned that the fisherman they had talked to the day before was NOT the captain of the ship. Indeed, the real captain was not at all interested in hosting tourists on his tuna boat, teachers or not. They were not welcome.

The next day, the tuna were gone. We girls found other things to explore, the crumbling wreck of a dory boat half buried in tidal sand, small dead sea creatures, ocean wrack, flotsam and jetsam.

In retrospect, the mystery of the tuna on the beach remains, though we have speculated over the years. It seems unlikely that those two tuna were headed to Rock Harbor (much easier to reach by boat, no need to haul them on shore). Was the false "captain" who accosted my parents trying to prevent them from noticing the fish were not headed for harbor and their usual market? Perhaps these were, in fact, *poached* tuna, meant for a black market fishery? It seems as if something, ahem, *fishy,* was going on. Still, our family got a close-up view of a kind of creature few of us ever encounter. Each of the two fish, stinking in a mist of sand fleas, was larger than the overturned fishing dory.

The giant black fish shedding scales on our beach were real. Mom and Dad were once eager to go deep sea tuna fishing.

We slept through it all.

by Pam Clements

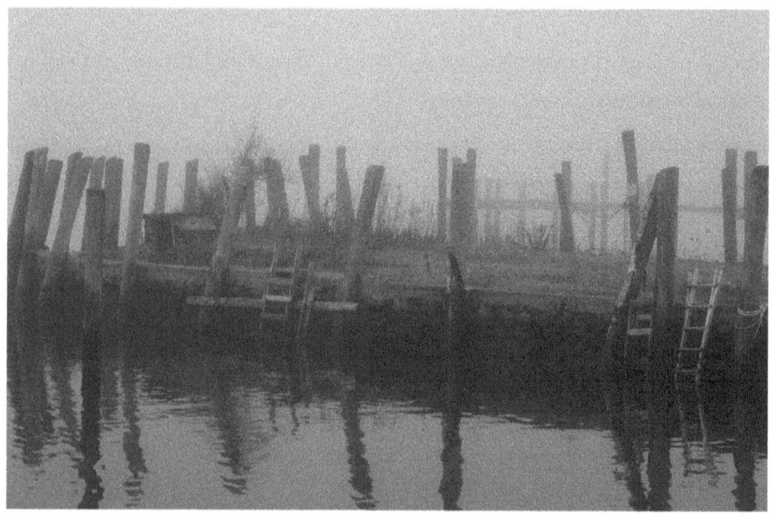

Paquachuck Morning by Midori Evans

He Built Tall Ships There

We forget that the root of the word "sacred" is not derived from any existing religion but rather an architectural feature called the "sacer," the name for a designed space, the interior domain of a Roman temple where one needed to be attentive to the needs of the gods. This is where the concept of "sacred" comes from. Outside of this space was the "profanum," unstructured real estate where one could do anything. —Adam Frank

It was winter on the Point. A line of weathered disco balls, whirling clockwise from a soggy puff of wind, caterpillared the shadowy space under the eaves of the Paquachuck Inn's wraparound porch. For some time since just past sunset, a woman was there, under the eaves, nestled like a bowling pin against the side of a musty overstuffed armchair and a deserted Huffy, waiting for the theologians.

They were former colleagues, the theologians. One Jewish, one Lutheran, both deeply devoted to books—to the reading of them, the teaching of them, the arguing about them. Confined to a curriculum under the ebb and flow of a semester, year in and year out, decade after decade, the theologians blended in with the other faculty, and happily so. But on seemingly random Wednesdays, they'd look a little different, for on those Wednesdays, they would argue.

The day would start out with early morning classes. Once over, with haste, they'd make their way to the racquetball courts. Neither man was athletic, per se, but furious were their games. Onlookers would wonder, aghast, really, at how these two colleagues, their affection and respect for each other well known, could be so brutal. The reality was while these two middle-aged academics were plumbing the depths of adrenaline reservoirs rarely touched since they left the womb, there was something equally as affecting, a phenomenon that has more to do with someone who clearly hasn't run in some time attempting to do so. For instance, consider the crosswalk. There's an awareness gained or disturbance had, at possibly a subatomic level, when a person who hasn't jogged or run for an extended period makes an attempt. Parts of their body move in ways that are now novel to them; gravity feels alien. Like a spotlight to the sleeping eye comes the sudden realization of an ass cheek set aloft. Or the non-negotiable presence discovered of the abdominal realm. Not to belabor the point, but of all the experiences one can spontaneously witness at a stoplight, this one phenomenon registers high on the list of the most spectacular and hilarious moments one can observe in the wild. It is also one of the most forgettable. Eventually, the light turns green, right?

After all this spectacle, the theologians would commence lunch. Always close to campus but routinely varying in location, they'd go through the motions of hydration, of mastication, of tip. But really, it was a ruse. What the theologians were actually doing was entering into a sacred space of their own creation, enabled by the social constructs surrounding things like a house salad and dressing on the side. See, they were now exhausted. Weary, really.

It's helpful at this point to review the history of employing physicality when it comes to matters of the mind. Yoga, for example, is widely considered to be a preamble to meditation. While yoga is widely practiced, few, however, follow through with the meditation part. Incidentally, to this point, Dr. Farr would often remark that going to yoga for just the exercise is like attending communion for the food and drink. But I digress. Aristotle took this care in a different direction, with his practice of lecturing while walking—the Peripatetic school. One cannot receive wisdom, he would argue, while sitting down; the body must be engaged, too!

What Doctors Farr and Svenson practiced was an improvisation of all of this, in that the racquetball allowed a systemic effect on the entirety of their anticipated exchange. Simply put, they were no longer pent up. They had sparred. The blood was flowing, but so, too, the calm. This receptive state would be furthered with fork-to-mouth movement while sitting. As for the decision to do this over lunch, rather than a snack or dinner, they were relying on the hard-wiring surrounding such a social engagement—what Daniel Kahneman considered part of the "slow" system of the brain. They were

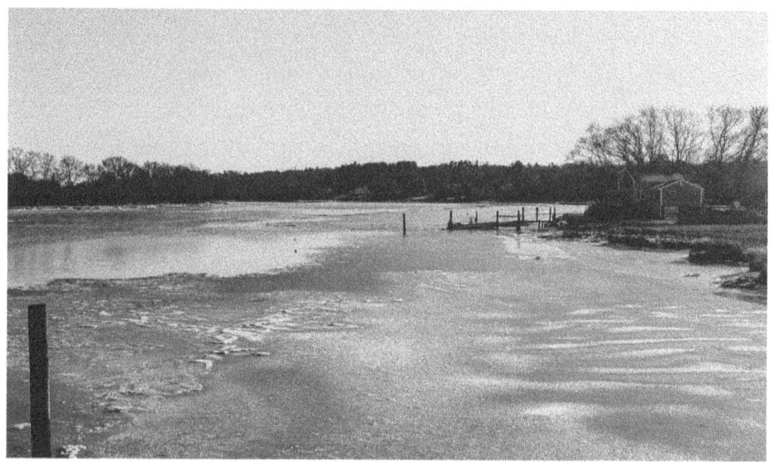

in public during the light of day. A cascade of social cues were set in motion that would, again, help ensure a civil rendering of what could become quite volatile. So baked into the environment were cues that subconsciously allowed for a further tempering. If your voice broke with the cadence of the din of the lunch chatter, it would not be helpful in the arguing, so the theologians thought.

After forty or so years, the theologians retired. One started blogging while writing a book. The other took to cooking, social media, and enjoying the unstructured lifestyle of the retired life. But there was, growing, an unease amongst them. Sure, they'd still have their lunches, but they wanted more. They began going on day trips. Instead of books, they'd rely on their shared experience of the day as both subject matter and physical exertion. And instead of lunch, they'd dinner. Soon this, too, grew stale, as they began to exhaust their surrounds. Day trips then turned into mini-vacations devoted to argument. This is how, one day, they happened upon Hixbridge Road and the story of the Cuffe shipyard that could be viewed from the bridge.

It started in the wine bar, during a tasting at Westport Rivers, where they overheard a couple of locals talking about the whalers that used to be built in shipyards running up the entirety of the east branch of the river.

"Excuse me," started Farr. Svenson, tall and clad in a bancha green bowtie, denim shirt, and houndstooth vest, punctuated the request with a quick, baritone-level moan, a supportive maneuver he was known for during his teaching days. Often, this was followed up with a quick inhale, hand-to-goatee placement, and then a dramatic nose exhale-softer moan combo suggesting a marination of thought was ensuing. This time, however, he freeformed the Chardonnay sample for a bouquet sniff instead.

Farr, with salt and pepper hair, kind, dark eyes, and browlined glasses, went on, "We don't mean to eavesdrop, but we just toured the Whaling Museum and now have just overheard you talking about whalers being built on this little river we drove over on our way here, is that right?"

"Kelly," chirped one of the tasting room staff, a woman with "Cheetah Jo" on her nametag. "We have a question from—" she paused, directing her gaze at Farr, to which he responded.

"Hi. Hello. We overheard you talking about building whaling ships on the Westport River."

Kelly, a thirty-six year old registered nurse with a pixie cut mane of chestnut-purple hair, was part of a group of six regulars parked around the short end of the rail. "That's right," she quipped, nodding with raised eyebrows. "And now we have people who can barely operate a kayak."

"Oh, that's harsh," responded one of the group, laughing a bit before taking another sip.

"Burn," said another, chuckling.

"Looks like we should keep this moving along before things get too intense here," Cheetah Jo added, while pouring the next wine.

"My sense is that they might not know much of the details we're looking for, uh, Cheetah Jo," Svenson quietly remarked.

"Ha!" she responded. "I forgot I had that name tag on. Yeah, I think you might have to head over to the speakeasy if you want a history lesson. I know that the crowd there likes to talk about things like that. And you'd like that place. It's on the Point. Make sure you slow down on the bridge and look down river along the shore. That was where Cuffe's shipyard was. He was a goddamn founding father. In my opinion."

"And the wine you so generously poured?" asked Farr.

"That's a bonus. Brandy made from our chardonnay, combined with freshly crushed chardonnay juice or 'must.' We barrel age this—neutral French— and when the time is right, we'll blend different vintages into this."

Both men took their last sips and moaned. "Smells like caramelized pineapple, Marcona almonds, and—"

"Lefse," Farr remarked.

"You said a 'founding father?'" asked Svenson.

"I did," replied Cheetah, with a twinkle in her eye.

"Those are powerful words. Looking forward to hearing more at the speakeasy," Farr declared while putting on his jacket.

"Down on the Point. At the Inn. You'll love it there."

Walking back to the rental car, the theologians decided that the day was full enough with the sightseeing and wine tasting, and that the speakeasy would be a gratuitous addition to an already perfect day. After all, they can do their research from afar and possibly return next year, if it feels right, if the mysteries take root.

by Corey Nuffer

Skipping Stones

Between Gooseberry Island
and Allen's Pond—ocean spray
East Beach—cobblestone and sand,
Gay Head south across the bay.

Smell of salty sea
mixed with brooding sky,
childhood memories carefree,
seagulls, seagulls catch my eye.

Slinging
spinning
skimming
skipping

Smooth, flat triangular rock,
shaped for bounce,
it will sail or plop
ounce for ounce.

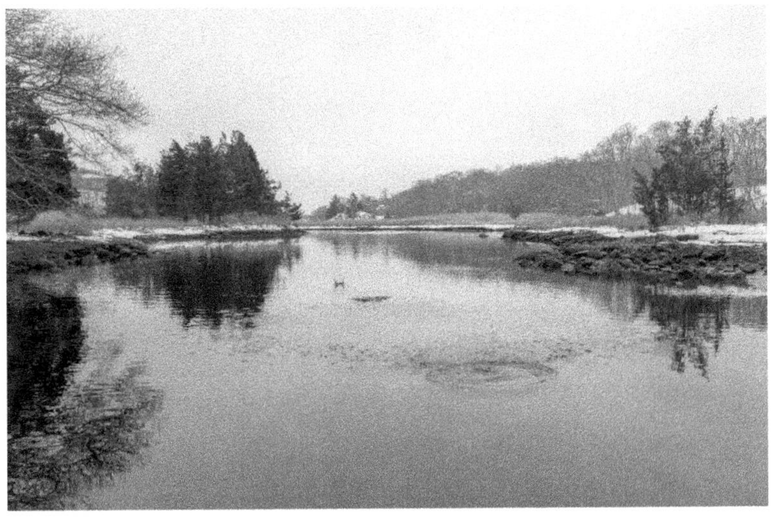

Slocum Skipper by Krista Allen

Look hard and dig deep,
sometimes it will soar across
or sink and lose its feet,
but try again, all is not lost.

Unmeasured by distance
skipping time and place,
these second chances,
little poems of grace.

Fling it, fling it,
free and wide-eyed,
throw it, throw it,
let it fly!

by Paul Mercier

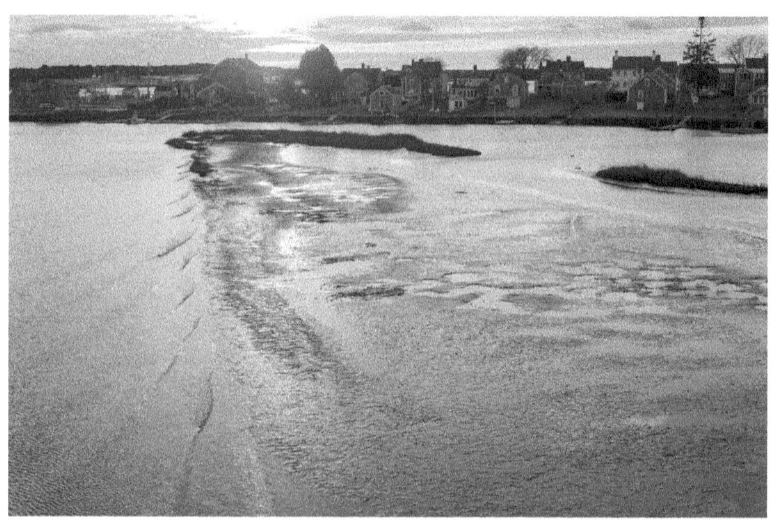

Westport Harbor by John Wojtowicz

Rockweed

In the late evening light, trucks roll over the grassy hill. Bumping and clanging along, Rebecca thinks, always the clanging. In the seat next to her sits her
husband of fifty years, the grey beard finally beginning to look distinguished
rather than the shock it was the first six years or so. His tanned arm juts out
the front window, right hand on the gear shift as he downshifts into second.
At the edge of the field, down along the water, people are chatting, alighting
from pick-up trucks, and already heading across the rocks. Ryan stands in
the back of a huge truck bed, throwing down what could be mistaken for
trash. Pellet layer bags, burlap sacks, old potato bags, coated plastic—all were
needed for gathering the rockweed.

The river's light sparkles in the gently diminishing sunset. A heavy bank of
blue clouds across the East Branch seems to be swallowing the shore. Bits of
tendrils trail off into the last yellow behind the clouds, illuminating strips of
water, shining on the women already topping off their first bags. Legs deep in
the water. Bending over with gloved hands to scoop off the best seaweed from
the high-set rocks just at tide's edge. Rebecca knows the routine: fifty-some
years of storing feed bags in the loft, her special waterproof gloves, the bit
of a body twist to get the seaweed to glide into the bag just so. And now the
need to pile the bags carefully in the inlet by the dock rather than trying to
carry them back herself, not anymore, not with her ancient bones. Early
in her marriage, only the men had come down to collect the seaweed. The
women gathered at the grange, rolling out pie dough and prepping the
brown bread. That changed decades ago. They work together on some tasks,
now, even if the majority of them still separate out along gender lines.

Rebecca and Tom park the truck off under the tree cover at the crest of the
hill. She clambers out into the overheated air and heads to unlatch the back
while Tom reaches under the front seat for the mosquito spray. Most years
they timed it pretty well; it was one thing to be slinging the bags up and onto
the truck bed when the mosquitos came out. Quite another to still have your
bags piled at the river and have to pass them down the human chain as the
mosquito invasion commenced. Off in the distance, a low humming motorboat makes its way along the docks that parallel Drift Road. Revving, then
quieting. It reminds Rebecca of the days she and Tom would go out on the
boat to lull Jacob to sleep. They'd follow the same route that motorboat was
on now—the narrow channel that zigzagged up the river, veering close to the
docks then back out to the deeper middle, up and around the rocky curve,

under the bridge, and finally up to the headwaters. Jacob would often be asleep by the time Tom turned around, Rebecca gazing in awe at the imposing stone acropolis in the nearby field.

Laughter echoes across the water now, so many hands and feet working in harmony, though each with their unique rhythm. Rebecca nods to Ed, half-waves to Danny's boy, the young one whose name she can never remember, then grabs three white burlap bags and wades in. Everything is slippery—the rocks, the rockweed, the muck at the bottom. People clamber over the rocks, step carefully through the tick-filled tall grasses, and skip the barnacle-encrusted shore rocks as best they can. Rebecca tries to imagine what it must have been like when her Quaker relatives first held the river-side clambake. Every year since 1887 this shindig has been going on. Back then it was held right at the river. They'd dig an enormous hole in the sand. Then pile up the clams, the tripe, the potatoes. The river would wash at the banks, swishing into the grass, crackling over the bits of fire it could swallow. But then the clams started to disappear, and the men got older. Too much work digging out all the clams yourself, Bernie had muttered one year, casting the last vote for letting the fishermen drive them in the day of.

All of a sudden it makes sense—the women staying back behind to do food prep—for who could possibly have waded into the river wearing the dresses they had way back then? Rebecca shakes her head as she looks at the younger women. So much has changed, not just the centuries. She would never be caught dead in shorts, much less the straight-up-to-the-edge-of-your-butt ones worn today. And this no-gender thing? Her great-grandchildren keep talking about it. Rebecca can't make heads or tails of it. In her mind, you are either a man or a woman. And that's that. Tom would shake his head slowly when she said things like that. She knew she had to force open her heart a bit more, or her great-granddaughter might stop speaking to her completely. It broke Rebecca's heart but they keep explaining to her that it makes Sandy happier. Happier? Since when did being a woman make you happier? Rebecca couldn't make rhyme or reason from the mess and most of the time preferred to just not think about it.

"Do you remember when she lost the chicken?" Rebecca hears Alison say as her fingers reach for another sweep of the slimy and knobbly black seaweed.

"I'm telling you, it's the John Deere!" Alex and Roberto are arguing about the best kind of tires for their tractor. The mallard duck family lets out a series of long quacks in frustration at the strangers swarming about their usually quiet and serene dinner table. Martin, shouting something indecipherable from the shore; Maina pointing at her wide-brimmed hat, firmly stuck on her head, wordlessly returning to her work. The rockweed slides through one's fingers, slopping over the edge of the bags, even ends up flinging through the air when one of the teenage boys gets a little rowdy. Every year, someone slips and falls, leaving them sloshing for the rest of the night in wet mud boots and not being allowed in for the end of the night tea.

"So sorry about your dog, Johnny," Rebecca says as she hands her first bag off. His high waders give him away as a clammer and Rebecca remembers reading about the lost dog on Facebook a few nights ago.

"Water's too high these days, ya know," he replies, no eye contact giving away the depth of his sorrow. Rebecca nods, glancing upriver to the bridge where the water flows just below the girders. Strange, for August, but then these rainstorms that come through are nothing like she remembers. Like a rain-swept tornado, they burst through in the late afternoon, practically drowning the cows by the feeding pen, pooling in places never before seen on the farm. She and Tom both purchased three sets of mud boots and rain parkas, storing extras in key spots around the property.

Rebecca turns her head, spotting her husband in his red hat. Down by the marsh grasses, the farthest away of anyone. Always a loner, Tom, he needs his quiet. She watches his aged body, still strong, bending and stuffing, twisting gracefully in the grass.

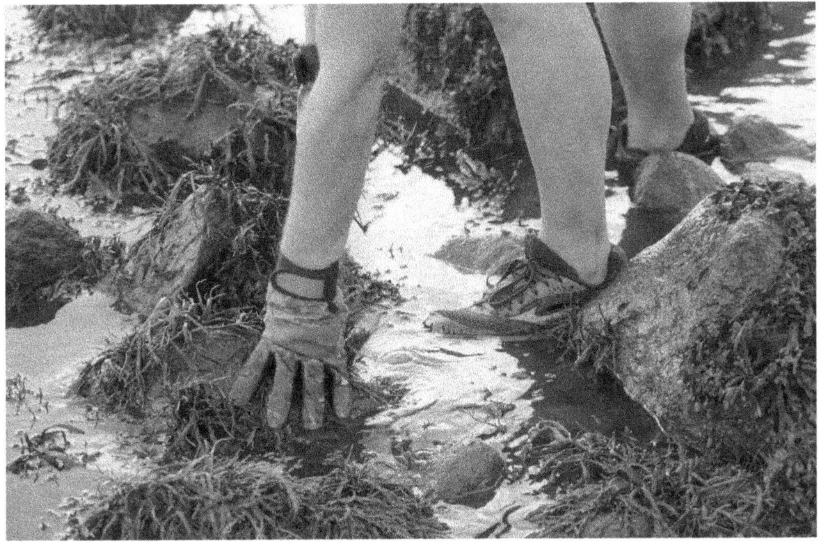

"Rebecca," Maina says, quietly. "Your friend is back." An osprey directly over Rebecca's head, long, slow sweeps, circling lower towards her and her companion. Years ago now, Rebecca had nursed a baby osprey, taking bits of fish down to the abandoned nest three times a day until the baby could feed itself. Every now and again, the osprey came to visit her when they encountered each other on the river. The bird dips and calls, hovering almost anxiously, until Rebecca stands fully erect, sets down her bags and opens her arms wide. Face up to the sky she chirps, high-pitched, making sure to leave enough time in between. The osprey chirps happily back then glides slowly away.

Ryan, one of the night's ringleaders, saunters by in the mud, easily carrying two bags of seaweed in hand with one more slung over his back. "Just about time to head back to the Meeting House!" he shouts. He throws his load onto the building pile and climbs into the truck to supervise. The light is trickling down to a dull blue-black. Three more men hop onto the truck, passing the wet bags to the back where Ryan swings them to the top of the pile to make more room. Tomorrow: another long day of clearing and laying out the fire and prepping the food. The rockweed comes on stage when the fire has built to a fever pitch and the stones are practically humming inside. That's when the wet, harvested seaweed inside all these bags pours out, layer after layer, making a steaming bubble of salt and water for cooking.

Thursday—always the third one in August—the crowds will make an appearance. Pouring out of cars, hopping out of pick-up trucks, walking from nearby farms. Curious neighbors and visitors will inch by in their cars because someone is using the mysterious corner plot of land that lies empty 364 days of the year. It's nothing to look at, the rest of the time. Shaded and unremarkable, carefully lined by a centuries-old stone wall, like almost every piece of property around here. Trees grow tall and untouched. They tower over the shed painted a faded robin's egg blue, the one with a pull-down metal gate that opens to two cement block windows. That shed is the center of all the activity but a mystery the rest of the year. All anyone sees is the desertion, never suspecting the crowd, seemingly appearing from nowhere, that graces its grassy hollows for one day in August.

The elders of the Meeting swear that God has a hand in the weather on clambake day. It's never too hot, never pouring rain. The worst they've had, they say, is a cloudy day where you couldn't see the sun shining through those glorious trees. Or, they would concede, the day when the junior fireman dropped his long pitchfork. It hit the ground with a bang; the wood pieces shot off hot embers while the hot coals bounced off and rolled, past a two-year-old resting in his stroller, past the pastor resting on the prayer bench, right on over to the stoves of the onion tender, resting his head as the onions boiled away, setting them on fire, scattering bits of onion everywhere. Except you couldn't blame that one on the weather gods.

The rest of the traditions remain: the recipe hanging on the Meeting House wall, the fire-tenders passing their jobs down to their sons and daughters, the exact ratio of cookies to quick breads at the sales tables. The regulars all show up in the early morning to give birth to the meal. Wrapping each individual sweet potato in its own shiny aluminum jacket; laying out the red plaid coasters on the rickety tables; a semicircle of hands reaching into wet buckets over and over again, tying handfuls of clams into individual mesh bags with one lone chef chopping the whitefish with a massive cleaver. The brown bread needs to be released from its mason jars. Pies retrieved and unstacked. Soon enough, though, the crowd will gather to watch the fire-tenders as they scoop the rocks, bury the coals, lay the rockweed, and plaster the wet sheets over the baking pile. Five hundred people—it does take some doing!—will give thanks in silence, one long minute passing impatient wishes up into the sunlit sky. As the rockweed pile gives up its baked treasures in wooden palletized boxes, the lonely long benches are filling. Seating forty to a bench, the guests are passing the brown bread baskets and being served coffee. The clambake hasn't truly begun, though. They are all eagerly awaiting the steaming baskets of clams, delivered by runners in sneakers, runners in aprons, runners in pigtails and fire-singed hair.

by Midori Evans

Ebb Tide

Night's Sister

Veronica

Before dawn in almost all seasons except the deep winter, Veronica heard the door bang and the strong smell of black coffee dissipate behind her husband as he headed off to ready the boat and check his pots. His parents had been lighthouse keepers back in the day when they kept vigil overnight, hurrying through the cold to replenish the kerosene. Now the lights were electric, and the old tower blinked at them ceaselessly from its empty perch on a rock.

He often woke up and paced the house at night as though his ancestors were biting at his heels. Veronica slept through his wanderings, but could tell what type of night it had been by the cast of his eyes the next morning—on a good day they were bright as the light darting out across the water, swift as a swallow. Other days they were obscured by a cloudy haze, the fog bell clanging from the darkness. On such days, he was like the rocks buried along the edge of the channel, and there was no telling how deep the waters ran.

Veronica had much time for reflection as she tidied their small cottage. She kept herself busy tending the garden, and had taught herself how to make repairs around the house and mow the lawn during his long stretches out on the water. She was not often idle. She was seldom lonely. If she ever did start to feel the tingle of melancholy, she started up her boxy Toyota Corolla and drove down to Jesse's house to visit with Miriam. The girl was nearly a woman now, yet there was something still so innocent about her. She always seemed to be in a dream state, never quite aware of her surroundings.

This morning, the shrubby juniper trees, curved in the memory of the wind, shook in the breeze. The dwarf white pines scattered their needles across the asphalt as it disappeared into sand. The fisherman's cottage where Miriam lived with her father was nestled behind the dunes, just a mile or so inland along the inlet. Veronica saw the girl framed in the window, sitting at the kitchen table with the end of her braid in her mouth. Her pencil was on the floor, and a book lay open before her.

Miriam

Miriam could hear the current from inside the small house she shared with her father—or at least imagined she could hear it. The water ripped through its channel, sometimes rising dangerously close to the edge. A kid from her school had drowned last year, thinking he could swim across it. He was a strong swimmer—they all were—but the ocean was stronger, especially when it was pinched into this small artery.

The dishes from breakfast sat forgotten in the sink, and Miriam's math homework was open on the opposite side of the table. The book in front of her was an anthology of poems by Edna St. Vincent Millay. Miriam startled at Veronica's knock on the door, and began to get up to open it, but sank back into her chair as the woman entered, bundled against the cold.

"Hi sweetie!" Veronica's voice was cheery. "Watcha doin?"

"Just reading." Miriam hastily picked up her pencil from the floor, and went to put the kettle on. "Do you want some tea?"

Veronica leaned over the page, reading the poem displayed on it.

Night Is My Sister, And How Deep In Love

Night is my sister, and how deep in love,
How drowned in love and weedily washed ashore,
There to be fretted by the drag and shove
At the tide's edge, I lie—these things and more:
Whose arm alone between me and the sand,
Whose voice alone, whose pitiful breath brought near,
Could thaw these nostrils and unlock this hand,
She could advise you, should you care to hear.
Small chance, however, in a storm so black,
A man will leave his friendly fire and snug
For a drowned woman's sake, and bring her back
To drip and scatter shells upon the rug.
No one but Night, with tears on her dark face,
Watches beside me in this windy place.

—Edna St. Vincent Millay

"Our young poet! I didn't know you read stuff like this. This was one of your mother's favorites, did you know that?" Veronica grabbed both of Miriam's shoulders and rubbed them affectionately.

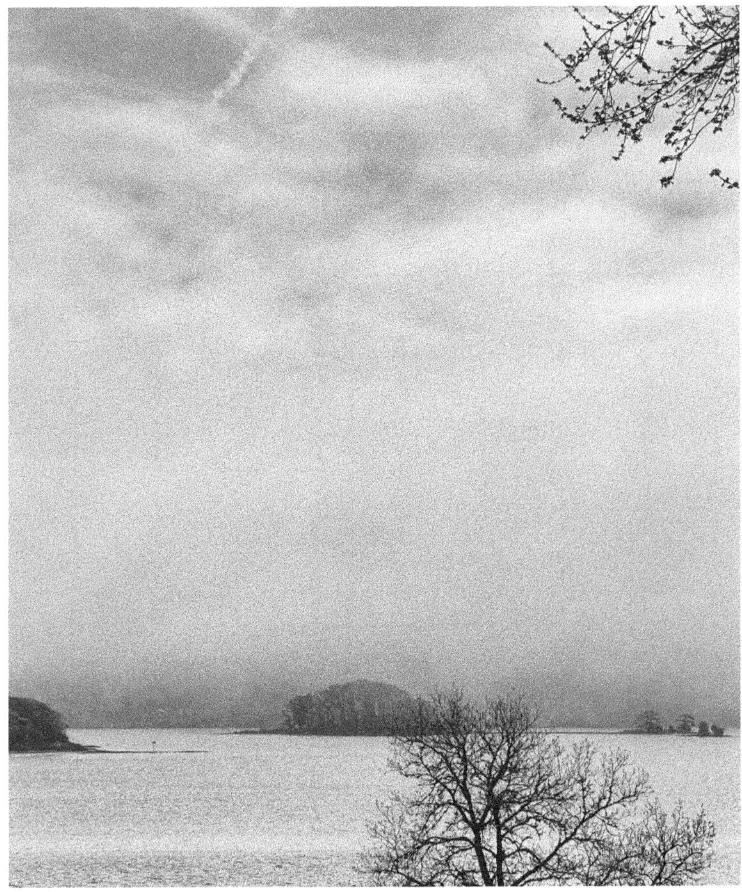

Fog Rising, East Branch by Lucy Bartholomay

"It was her book." Miriam turned to the inside front page where Celeste's name was inscribed in a careful cursive.

"What's this?" Veronica flipped the book closed to reveal a notebook beneath, covered in writing.

"Nothing," Miriam swept it hastily closed and onto her lap.

"Come on, I'd love to read it! Is that a story you're working on?"

"It's not ready." Miriam blushed, got up abruptly, and shoved the notebook into the side of the couch cushion. "Could you help me with my math homework? I don't understand the next problem."

"Sure. I'll try."

Miriam's mother had been one of the few friends Veronica had been able to make in this town. New Englanders were as cold as their surroundings, loyal towards their own but notoriously suspicious of outsiders, and they still treated her with a guarded suspicion, even after she'd lived here for nearly thirty years. But Celeste was different. She had the wildness of the sea and the hearty core of a northerner, but she was quick to love, welcoming to any who crossed her path. She was always and forever on an impetuous quest to experience a thrill. The two women could not have been more different when they met, just barely into their twenties, but Veronica found herself swept into Celeste's intoxicating glow. She was always ready to try most things, be it skinny dipping, cooking up a rock crab pulled from a lobsterman's bycatch, or a line of white powder from a stranger at the local bar.

Jesse was handsome back in the day—charming, even, in his gruff and soft spoken way, but he landed Celeste not with his charm but through an age-old blunder. Veronica was not surprised when Celeste revealed that she was pregnant, but she was by how wholeheartedly Celeste embraced this new reality. Eventually she realized that for Celeste this was another thrill, another experience to fling herself into, without thought of consequence, until the next thing came along to grab her attention.

Poor Miriam—the girl was getting too old to believe the same recycled story Jesse had been repeating all these years. And yet—maybe she was better off than if she knew the truth.

The kettle blared and the two dark heads bent over the homework on the table. To anyone driving by, they would appear as mother and daughter, not two childless and motherless women.

Miriam got up to go to the bathroom, and knowing she would take a long time with whatever mysterious teenage rites she performed in there, Veronica darted to the couch and pulled out the notebook. In tiny handwritten letters that tilted down the page was written:

The Selkie

The light filters down, shifting to the depths. I remember the feeling of it on my dry skin like a distant dream. The taste of a fresh fruit, juice running down my chin, and the liquid on my lips, strangely flavorless.

On certain midsummer nights when there is a full moon illuminating the sky, turning the night bright as day, we seals come ashore and shed our skins, transforming into humans.

I remember the feeling of nakedness, a cold deep to the bone, deeper than the water which now cradles me. Searching for my skin on the slippery rocks, feeling only the sharpness of barnacles and the slick oily seaweed.

My sisters stop their song and slip back into the water. I wade in after them, but when I submerge, I feel a pressure rushing up my nostrils, like someone is stabbing me inside. A terrible pressure. I cannot close my nose to it. I surface again, sputtering. My sisters circle, their heads popping up out of the water, watching me with their large, dark eyes. Then one by one, they disappear, as I hear a hoarse mumbling behind me, and the shape of a man, a young fisherman with a wiry beard trimmed neatly around his smooth chin.

His eyes were kind but what I remember most vividly is the sense of loss. The intervening time, when I lived as a human, breathing air and sharing the cot of that human man, is like a blur of color. A million moving shapes, kelp dancing in the current. A cacophony of sounds, the sharp cry of a small pup with eyes like his. So many sounds—except for my sisters' songs.

I tried to return to the sea many times, wading in up to my neck. Each time a wave would push me under, that same suffocation. The will to live pushed me back above the surface, stumbling back onto the sand with my spindly flippers.

One day, when the man was gone, the small pup found my skin. Her eyes sparkled and glittered, the feeling on her hands was so smooth. For me to feel it was to breathe again. To feel warmth, like the sun shining for the first time. I waited until nighttime and slid it back on, once more whole.

Beneath, in an open handed print, was scrawled: *Seal mothers and their pups can recognize each other through unique calls.*

Veronica

Veronica felt her eyes tingle with unfamiliar tears. Memories surfaced unbidden: Celeste, shrieking with delight, running into the surf and diving fluidly under the oncoming waves while Veronica waded behind her, barely keeping her footing. Celeste, her figure lithe and trim, taking the rudder to guide the boat into harbor, while Veronica watched dumbly. Celeste, her tousled head resting on Jesse's shoulder for the first time, while Veronica pushed down a hot and searing jealousy.

So this is the explanation Miriam had come up with for the complete absence of her mother from her life? Veronica remembered watching *The Secret of Roan Innish* with her when she was a child, and introducing her to the legend of the selkies—seal maidens who came ashore and transformed

into humans, who sometimes had their skins stolen and their hearts captured by an enterprising man. Veronica felt another surprising jealousy: she
wished that she could have come up with this explanation herself. To explain
Celeste's absence, Jesse had chosen to call her dead, and Veronica had gone
along with it all these years, not knowing what else to do. But how was she to
tell Miriam that her mother was not dead, nor magical—simply gone? She
couldn't. Not after all these years.

The Selkie

Down at the mouth of the inlet, where the strong current pushed against the
tide, white capped waves swirling into unpredictable shapes, a few dark heads
broke the surface of the water. The seals bobbed up and down, their huge
dark eyes surveying the shore.

by Heather Claire Meehan

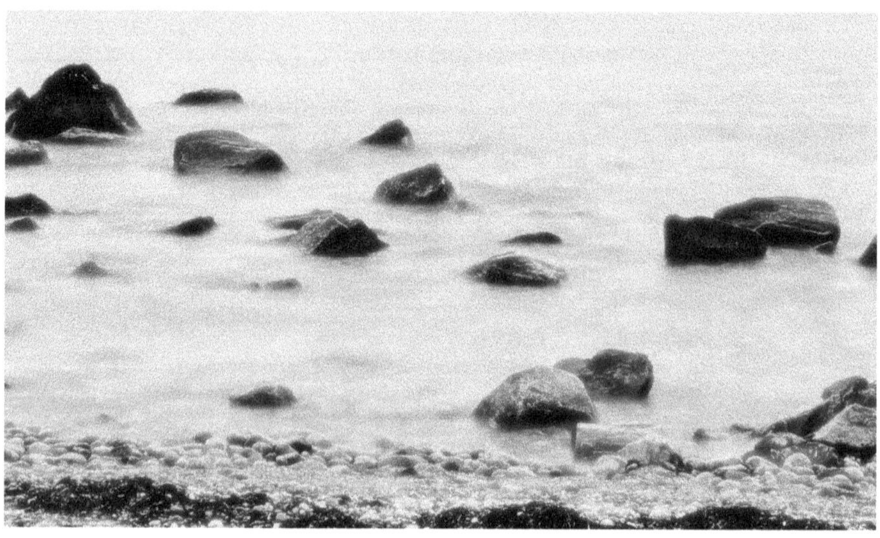

East Beach by Steven Ashley

Clearing Cloudy Water

I had an answer, a solution. I *"marveled at the heart divining, at the hand designing."**

I have looked for answers in books, drawings, and poetry most of my life. I thought about the times I wished to glom a slice of clarity in my borrowed books. I would steal a slice of security—a slice of confidence. On every trip around the sun, I have had days when I felt despondent, adrift, and out of my depth. There was no warning; it blew in when the wind was driving from the northeast. It was like a chunk of driftwood appearing from a busted-up dory from an outlying cerulean sea.

My heart felt heavy. My breathing was shallow. My joints were a wee bit stiffer. I questioned everything as I sat where the west branch of our river collided with the channel. There was no rhythm to the day. I couldn't swim to my destination of choice, to the place I needed to be, or where I had chores to complete.

The water was dense, dark, and like a forest at dusk. Obstacles bobbed up and down. I looked at the other swimmers, the other players in life. They had inherited something; they wore it like a sheen on smooth skin. I didn't know if it was by luck or destiny. They were swifter. They were cleverer. They were propelled by something that came before them. It hurt to look at them. Their lithe bodies torpedoed through what appeared to be the clear waters of their lives. It was a silly view. I portended a coming storm.

My journey was through cloudy water, churning and roiling. My journey was burdened by the thick, wet blue jeans of my life clinging to my legs and leaden shoes that helped me walk to nowhere. My journey was burdened by the compass that couldn't read true north.

I was surprised I hadn't sunk yet. If I succumbed to falling, it would have been a bludge. I would have let go of my determination, my grit, my fortitude, and sheer will. I would have tumbled down slowly. Perchance I would have relished the ride.

No. I stayed afloat. I grabbed a piece of the busted-up dory. I had a hint of its provenance. It was from a distant but familiar sea. My nature kept me afloat. It kept me trying. It kept me kicking and grabbing for life with the

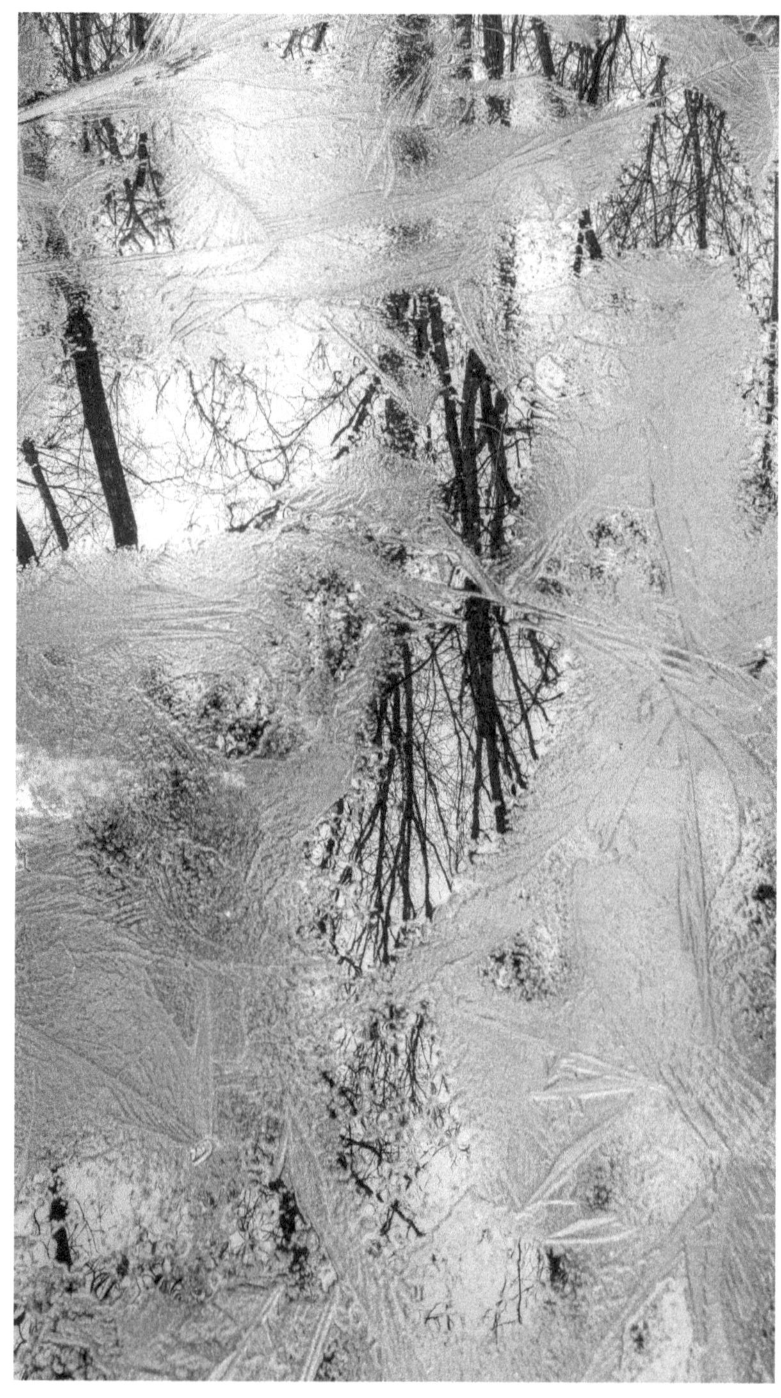

Frosty Reflections by Rich Castenson

strokes of my strong arms. My nature allowed me to push away the debris, clear the cloudy water with my breath, and kick off the heavy boots and sodden blue jeans.

My nature, where my heart and hand worked in concert, had surfaced. The drunken dissonance had captured my limbs and arms and suffocated me. At last, it dissipated. It was scattered into fine particles. It would become the plankton on the ocean floor of life. I no longer saw the other swimmers. I was focused and caught in the draft and propulsion of my stroke and the bluish haze of water. I would accomplish what I needed to do. I was free. I knew the time would come when I would again wish to grasp some clarity in my borrowed books from that place that houses sense and sensibility. I will have starved myself of calm and quiet.

I sat and waited. The wind stilled; the halyards stopped clanging as the lone gull with its long notes went in for a dive. I *"marveled at the heart divining, at the hand designing."** My answer. My solution.

a quote from Hildegarde von Bingen, b.1098 German Abbess, writer, philosopher, mystic and poetess

by Heidi O'Donnell Eastman

Soulful Tide

I wear this salty embrace like a favored sweater, wading comfortably through rows of shallow warm waves over rippled sand. It is the perfect fit on a perfect day, and I breathe deeply as the late afternoon sun reveals a magical sparkling path to the horizon. My skin is singed from this long, hot day, and I should leave, but I just can't let go.

Because this faint, tight burn is a welcome shift from the emptiness of loss. As I walk, a forgotten sandcastle surrenders to the tide, causing me to wonder what will be left of me when grief has had its fill.

The ocean gives and it takes away. Like life, which recently claimed my oldest child. Both are indiscriminate breakers of hearts. While hope rises with each promising dawn, the setting sun bleeds memory over these waters, a knife cut of cinematic brilliance.

As the golden hour nears, I see the silhouette of a figure in the distance, and my mind plays tricks. I think I can faintly hear the explosive joy of my son's laugh on the breeze. Of course, it is not him. I know I would like to hear it. But I raise my hand in acknowledgment anyway.

This historic spit of rocky sand is the keeper of history. The precious threads of my life's fabric are now divided into moments of before—during—and after.

Before, teenage summers were about hitchhiking to Chandy's for clam cakes and Cokes and broiling all day on boiling sand. It was learning to drive a stick shift in this parking lot, sneaking beer, and the terror of running into eels everywhere but in bath and seawater.

During was overflowing buckets of beach toys, cries for ice cream, and battling the undertow, car sickness, and thunderstorms. It was chasing gulls that tried to steal our picnic dinners and the great collapsing beach chair tale that never got old.

And then came the call that changed our lives and where the after began. Where the reality of loss, and the memory of love, is imprinted on each season and each rolling wave. And where the relentless ache of a mother's heart is not washed away but salved in the inevitable rhythm of the ebb and flow.

This longtime ocean friend offers the gift of solace in the symphony of gulls, the crack of waves on rock, and the scent of salt, seaweed, and sunblock.

This shared history allows tender memories of the before and during to soften the struggle to move forward as the after continues to evolve.

Here, in this place, the threads of this ongoing love story will always be mine. Though gone, here, the essence of this child will always share it.

by Michele Morgan Bolton

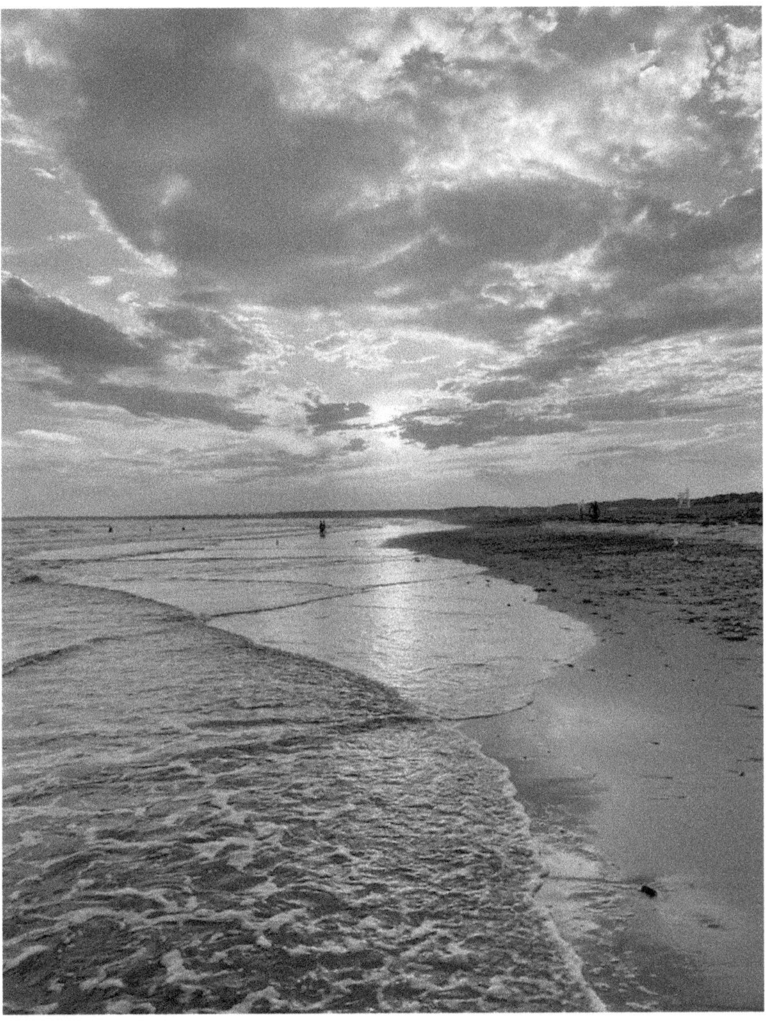

Reminiscence by Michele Morgan Bolton

The Memory of a Ship

The King of ships once you were
Wailing waters far and near
Carrying passengers here and there
Sailing seas everywhere

Your sails were trim
Your roping tight
In day you would swim
And float by night

You knew each man bits and bets
They confided their sea bound secrets
Their hopes and dreams lived 'neath your sails
Many feet and hands passed your rails

Now it's over; that was it
Alone in the shallow you sit
Wrecked, ever bound to tarry
No whales to hunt no people to ferry

Left in the sandy shallows waiting
Weather has worn you down, grating
Your great sails no longer stand straight
But yet there is a beauty in your fate

A ship slowly decays and dies
Knowing it takes with it
More memories
Than you or I…

by Kathryn Lee Hamilton

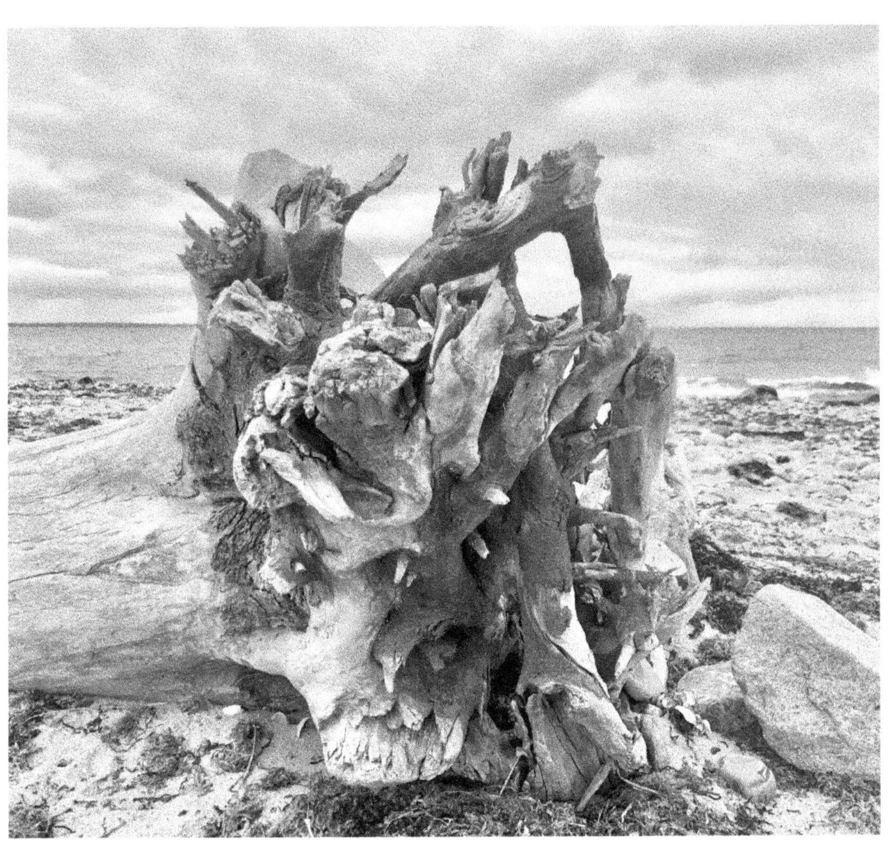

Storm Leftovers by Carolyn Edwards

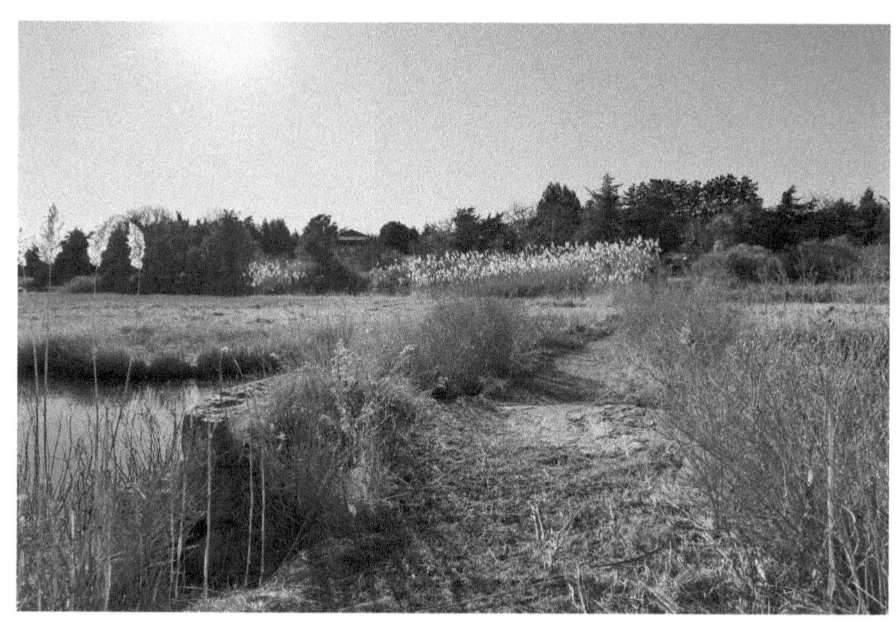

Cow Path-3, Westport Point by Charles Eastman

The Water's Edge

It's an ancient cow path, an old easement,
along which a farmer would drive a cattle herd to
some edible grasses, a single file
that often meandered. A farmer's dog,
a small, nimble and fleet shepherd, would do
to keep the cows in line, if not content,
until they reached the pasture. It's no trial
but if the ground's wet, it could be a slog.

The farmer, at the bovine parade's end,
would be on or near an old bridge of stone
which spans an estuary that still flows
into a tidal flat, and from there to
the Westport River. Standing there alone,
he'd see the pasture (at times used to mend
the nets of fishermen); like them he knows
what salt and water allow him to do.

Cattails and cordgrass set the water's edge
while red fescue and switchgrass mark the meadow.
Now, on a winter's day, a lower sun
distinctly lights this bleak cradle of life.
The spongy path and my stiff steps foreshadow
a fallen world where this scene and its pledge
of ebb and flow is at risk and my own run
faces the implacable subsidence of life.

by James Cronin

"The Water's Edge" was inspired by a collaboration
with Charles Eastman and his black and white photographs of the site.

An Ode to Horace

It's funny how images collide and stories are born of a kaleidoscope of memories we sense but can't quite see. We feel our stories deep inside as facts and figures push through the fog of the pile-up of daily events. The days become weeks, the weeks become years and suddenly we are looking at the trajectory of a life navigated far longer than the tack ahead.

I have always indulged a compulsion to keep old things. Perhaps this is driven by a desire to be remembered myself. More accurately, as an adopted child, there is a need to create a context of belonging to some particular herd defined by their collected histories and stories. At first the outsider, I find I am now the curator.

Just the other day, three 3-cent stamps on a yellowed envelope changed my trajectory dramatically. Going through forgotten family "waterscapes" to inform this story, I came across pictures of my 9-year-old only brother holding a baby that could only be me! Till that moment I had cobbled together "my earliest memories" starting at age two. The brown envelope from *Sharrow Por-*

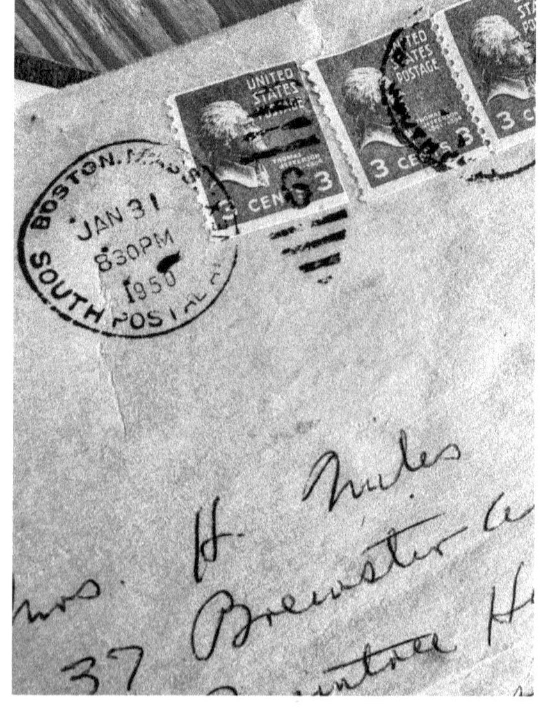

trait Photographers in Brookline was dated Jan 31, 8:30pm 1950. I was 6 months old. Were they test driving me? Or was that part just a blur? I am losing the plot—or maybe just seeing it. This is about water. It's learning to float with my adopted family. Becoming a safe harbor of belonging through stories for my children and theirs.

Here's a picture of Dad learning to sail in Coronado, CA. I love that grin and saw it on New Year's Eve when I ran along Horseneck Beach with my brother's grandkids, ages 6 and 4. We hardly know each other but that

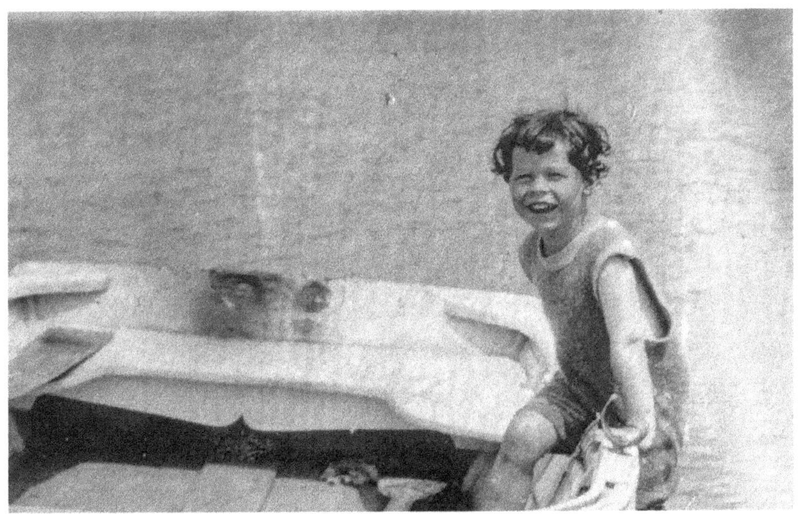

"Miles" grin is unmistakable. "Here's some shells, Annnnt Lorna!" A fierce competition has erupted between the small siblings each filling my pockets with shell shards and horseshoe crab shell remnants. Dad's grin and giddy love for the sea ebullient in these two little sea rats.

Born in San Diego, Dad lived down the road from the del Coronado Hotel near the Coronado Shores, Marinas and Cays. A generation later, when I was a child, we lived here in New England by the sea in the summertime. Our weatherbeaten cottage at the end of a dirt road was a two-minute walk to the beach, crossing just one paved road. We'd arrive, open the car doors and the cocker spaniels would bolt down the lane and return exuberantly stinking of fish. Our little house was well stocked with tomato juice for such occasions and my mom's impromptu Bloody Mary brunches.

Even before I could walk, I experienced the waves from the safety of my father's broad shoulders. As a wartime hydraulic engineer, he knew everything about water. All kinds of water. The water content of clouds, their colors related to the sun, and the patterns waves make on the sandy shore. Decades later I learned from my brother that Dad knew a lot about submarines, too, only that he couldn't share that knowledge with *anyone*. I assumed my brother knew and just wasn't telling me. After all, he was there first…

When I was little (and walking) Dad taught me to let go and float. I felt confident that the strength of his fingers at the nape of my neck would give me stability in the face of oncoming waves. Still today, when turbulence threatens me or my family, I remember how Dad taught me to float. That memory of leaning into the waves carries me through most anything.

My cocker Gracie and I explore the Westport beaches nearly every day between mid-September and April. Those feelings that skate across my mind —the Dad memories—almost always accompany us on our walks. I seek out the sine curves, repeating patterns left by the incoming waves no matter what their size, shape or force. In summertime, I point to these mysteries for my two children and now for my 4 grandchildren and their 2 cousins.

This week I have been thinking a lot about the continuity of landscapes— some seen and some unseen. It is there for me, for my family, and all of us when we take time to look, to connect, to remember, to see and honor our places in this continuing story. The landscapes remind us of *us*, our stories and where we started. The stories bind us to each other, past and present. The waves may shift the shape of the plot, but the memories endure, safely encased in these stories of the sea about us.

I'm sure my father saw equations where I can see only perfection in the evenly placed zigs and zags. In the constancy of the ocean and the relentless-ness of those waves, I feel his presence again and again. I look up from time to time and he is there with these magical great grandchildren, each holding my hand, each others' hands, and his.

by Lorna Miles

Acknowledgments

Author and Photographer Biographies

Krista Allen is an author and artist living in Westport, MA.

Steven Ashley recently retired from a 50-year career in public TV. He lives full-time in Westport and has returned to photography including capturing B&W landscapes.

Lucy Bartholomay is a Westport artist. Taking pictures helps her see relationships in the spaces around her and informs how she creates her work.

Michele Morgan Bolton weaves relatable personal experiences into essays and fiction and loves to capture the magic of everyday moments in images.

Rich Castenson photographs to capture artistic images and interesting moments in time.

Pam Clements lives in Albany, New York where she writes about the natural world and the human condition.

Deb Coderre lives near Freetown Forest where she finds inspiration for her writings about nature, people, and the life we all share.

Mark L. Collins writes nature-inspired prose, drawing from Tagore and Emerson to explore divine connections through natural beauty in his literary works.

James Cronin, after a career in law, took up poetry and has published two books: World of Shadows (2018) and The Mortal Angels (2024).

Susan Czernicka is still writing, still painting, still drawing … and still awe-struck.

Charles Eastman is a photographer and architectural designer who co-owns Belle Maison Westport, an arts venue and studio.

Heidi O'Donnell Eastman is an artist and writer and teaches at RISD. She co-owns Belle Maison Westport, an arts venue and studio.

Carolyn Edwards photographs urban scenes, landscapes, people, and nature while looking for emotion, the unexpected, and the unusual.

Midori Evans loves creating meaning and connections in her work as a creativity coach, writer, and photographer. She is the founder of Midori Creativity and the Westport Writers Group.

Shara Grant is a Westport native who photographs nature and anything else that captures the eye in her travels about the backroads of Westport.

Margot Green grew up in Bass River, South Yarmouth, MA. She has lived year round in Westport since 1995.

Melinda Green has snapped photos from her daily swims for the past five years and can't bear to delete them.

Kathryn Lee Hamilton grew up in the basement of the Museum of Fine Arts Boston. This childhood experience has greatly influenced her imagination and writing.

Eve Lesses is an LICSW psychotherapist who loves her work, improv theater, dance, the supportive collegiate atmosphere of the WWG, and living near the sea.

Joan V. McKinley has a deep love for the Westport River where she and her husband enjoyed beautiful sunsets and taught their sons to sail.

Heather Claire Meehan is a writer and farmer who finds inspiration in the changing seasons of a tidal landscape.

Paul Mercier is a lifelong student who has been writing and workshopping poetry since 2013.

Lorna Miles has led communications offices at Johns Hopkins, Brandeis, and the US Holocaust Memorial Museum in Washington D.C. She writes fiction and memoir.

Corey Nuffer is the In-House Storyteller for Kevin Cradock Builders and Mill Shop, edits at Spinner Publication, and co-leads SouthCoast Almanac's Walking Book Tours.

Diane Pienta is devoted to nature, beauty, creativity and connection. She writes to shine a light on the everyday magic all around us.

Ed Reiss is a sailor who notes that his photography captures the water's ever-changing moods, reflecting its beauty, peace, and the deep connection it inspires.

Aaron Smith has chased academic degrees and career advancement. Now he just wants to sit quietly and write stories.

Frederick Thurber is a writer from South Dartmouth who formally published a weekly nature/science column in the Westport Shorelines newspaper.

Stefanie Toner captures the magic of everyday moments in her photography. She weaves life's stories through the camera lens, revealing emotion, light and authenticity.

John Wojtowicz has appreciated the (mostly) tranquil environment of Westport since childhood. Long enough to have seen some significant changes, but the breezes and tides are always there.

Information about the Westport Writers Group

The Westport Writers Group is a diverse and wide-ranging group of writers from across the SouthCoast, MA and RI geographic area. We gather to share our stories, expertise, and writing. Contact us for more information at westportwritersmass@gmail.com.

Information about Midori Creativity

Midori Creativity is growing a nurturing and inclusive creative ecosystem through community projects, coaching, workshops, and creative inspiration. Visit midoricreativity.com for more information or to get involved.

Thank you to Our Local Sponsors

It's wonderful to live in a place that supports the arts and cares about community. We are so grateful for the local sponsors who have generously supported this project.

Butterfly Effect Farm, Westport

Gooseberry Natural Foods, Westport

Westport Federal Credit Union

Anonymous

And a personal donation in memory of Alexander G. Morgan Bolton

We would like to thank Allen's Neck Friends Meeting for their support as well as the Massachusetts Cultural Council, the Westport Cultural Council, the Dartmouth Cultural Council, and the Westport Friends Meeting for their roles in keeping us all writing and creating.

www.ingramcontent.com/pod-product-compliance
Lightning Source LLC
Chambersburg PA
CBHW040130150726
48005CB00015B/2442